ROUTLEDGE LIBRARY EDITIONS:
PSYCHOLOGY OF EDUCATION

Volume 47

LEARNING THEORY AND BEHAVIOUR MODIFICATION

LEARNING THEORY AND BEHAVIOUR MODIFICATION

STEPHEN WALKER

Routledge
Taylor & Francis Group
LONDON AND NEW YORK

First published in 1984 by Methuen & Co. Ltd

This edition first published in 2018
by Routledge
2 Park Square, Milton Park, Abingdon, Oxon OX14 4RN

and by Routledge
605 Third Avenue, New York, NY 10017

Routledge is an imprint of the Taylor & Francis Group, an informa business

British Library Cataloguing in Publication Data
A catalogue record for this book is available from the British Library

ISBN: 978-1-138-24157-2 (Set)
ISBN: 978-1-315-10703-5 (Set) (ebk)
ISBN: 978-1-138-63488-6 (Volume 47) (hbk)
ISBN: 978-1-315-20662-2 (Volume 47) (ebk)

Publisher's Note
The publisher has gone to great lengths to ensure the quality of this reprint but points out that some imperfections in the original copies may be apparent.

Stephen Walker

Learning Theory and Behaviour Modification

Methuen

London and New York

To Alison and Ruth-Mary

First published in 1984 by
Methuen & Co. Ltd
11 New Fetter Lane, London EC4P 4EE

Published in the USA by
Methuen & Co.
in association with Methuen, Inc.
733 Third Avenue, New York, NY 10017

Typeset by Rowland Phototypesetting Ltd
Bury St Edmunds, Suffolk
Printed in Great Britain by
Richard Clay (The Chaucer Press) Ltd
Bungay, Suffolk

British Library
Cataloguing in Publication Data

Walker, Stephen
Learning theory and behaviour modification. –
(New essential psychology)
1. Educational psychology
2. Behaviour modification
I. Title II. Series
370.15 LB1051

ISBN 0-416-33810-0

Library of Congress
Cataloging in Publication Data

Walker, Stephen F.
Learning theory and behaviour modification.
(New essential psychology)
Bibliography: p. Includes index.
1. Learning. 2. Behavior modification.
I. Title. II. Series.
LB1060.W34 1984 370.15'23
83-19475
ISBN 0-416-33810-0 (pbk.)

Contents

1

Introduction to learning theory

At some point, anyone reading this must have acquired a tendency to convert letters into sounds, and to associate strings of letters with the meanings of words. We cannot be certain exactly how this happened, but there is surely no doubt at all that it involved learning from experience. There may be some aspects of human language that remain uninfluenced by individual experience, but the spoken words I am using here are a result of my having learned English. There are many other languages which could be written with the same script, such as French or Spanish, but anyone who reads Russian, Greek or Hebrew will have had to learn a different set of visual signs as the alphabet, while the Arabic script is even more unfamiliar, and reading (or writing) in ancient Egyptian or Chinese is a different kettle of fish altogether.

Thus, the use of language requires a strong element of learning, and so does the knowledge of social custom and ritual, and all beliefs, loyalties and values that can be shown to differ from one culture to another, or from one generation to the next. And in many cases, it is quite obvious that even in the same culture or sub-culture one family may differ from another, or one person from another person, because of previous tragedies or traumas that may produce either weakness or strength of personality. More positively, they may differ because of family traditions or personal histories of practice and determination that may transmit or develop skills and expertise – whether musical, muscular or social.

Whether in academic education, specialized training, or in the more informal and unconscious adaptation to social and personal circumstances, there has always been a case to make that human life is largely dependent on individual learning – it is the flux, not the fixity, of human technologies and social institutions which most distinguishes our species from any other. Therefore, those who believe that they have found general laws, or universal principles, which apply to learning have often gone on to infer that the same general laws must underlie wider areas of human psychology, and can be used as general principles of human behaviour. The idea that the same theory can apply to all learning has often been attacked, both by those who think that innate factors determine human nature and by those who reject any 'reductionist' approach which tries to find underlying explanations for the complexities of life.

In spite of such criticisms, there are two quite separate reasons for continuing to study learning theories. The first is that this is still a vigorous research area, with technical advances in the design of experiments producing new answers to some of the old puzzles (Rescorla, 1980; Dickinson, 1980). The second is that the old theories themselves, despite numerous logical and metaphysical difficulties, have spawned a collection of practical measures, known as behaviour modification, or behaviour therapy, which have made a significant contribution to such areas as the treatment of severe neurotic phobias and the education of retarded or handicapped children.

The development of learning theory

Darwin

As I am writing in the centennial of the year of Darwin's death – 1882 – it is appropriate to acknowledge the Darwinian roots of some of the features of learning theories. In the conclusion to *The*

Origin of Species, Darwin says: 'In the distant future I see open fields for far more important researches. Psychology will be based on a new foundation, that of the necessary acquirement of each mental power and capacity by gradation' (Darwin, 1859/1968, p. 458). A new foundation for psychology exactly like this seems distant still, and an emphasis on the gradual evolution of mental powers and capacities is not really a characteristic of the theories I shall shortly review. But it is obvious that the Darwinian theory of evolution emphasizes the continuity of human and animal psychology, and the use of evidence from laboratory experiments on animal learning to test principles and specific hypotheses of supposedly wider application could almost be used as a definition of a learning theory.

In *The Descent of Man* (1871/1901) Darwin has two chapters on 'Comparison of the mental powers of man and the lower animals' whose aim is 'to show that there is no fundamental difference between man and the higher mammals in their mental faculties' (p. 99). Much of these is taken up with anecdotal evidence for the existence of wonder, curiosity, complacency and pride, as well as reason, abstraction and imagination, in mammals such as the baboon and the domestic dog. The conclusion is that 'The lower animals differ from man solely in his almost infinitely larger power of associating together the most diversified sounds and ideas' (Darwin, 1871/1901, p. 131), and 'We must admit that there is a much wider interval between one of the lowest fishes, as a lamprey or lancelet, and one of the higher apes, than between an ape and man' (p. 99). These assertions are used by Darwin to support his theory that human abilities could have evolved gradually from those of related species, rather than to forward the 'new foundation' for psychology which he had referred to earlier. However, by identifying the power of associations as a critical factor in human intelligence and firmly relating human mental capacities to those of animals, Darwin prepared the way for later 'associationist' theories about psychology which derive supporting evidence from animal experiments.

Pavlov and the conditioned reflex

When, in 1882, Darwin was buried in Westminster Abbey, a leader in *The Times* expressed full appreciation of his work. But, when

The Descent of Man first appeared in 1871, *The Times* had thundered that 'morality would lose all elements of stable authority' if the public were to believe it. Few today suggest that the theory of natural selection (or in the case of *The Descent of Man*, sexual selection) is a threat to public order, although neither the religious Right nor the political Left have much enthusiasm for modern varieties of Darwinism such as sociobiology (Wilson, 1975).

Another branch in the roots of learning theory also ran into ideological resistance early on. In 1866 the St Petersburg Censorial Committee banned a popular book, and prosecuted its author for undermining public morals. The author was neither a pornographer nor a political theorist, but a physiologist called Sechenov, and the book was *Reflexes of the Brain*, which introduced the controversial suggestion that 'all acts of conscious or unconscious life are reflexes'. Perhaps the authorities were especially sensitive, 1866 being the year of the first assassination attempt on Alexander II, but the case against Sechenov soon collapsed, and *Reflexes of the Brain* later made a deep impression on the young Ivan Pavlov (Gray, 1979).

Pavlov (1849–1936) was awarded a Nobel prize in 1904 for his work on digestion. In the lecture he gave in Stockholm when he received it, he described some of his findings as 'conditioned reflexes', although many of the more detailed experiments were to come later, as Pavlov became less concerned with digestion, and more concerned with 'an investigation of the physiological activity of the cerebral cortex' (the subtitle to Pavlov's *Conditioned Reflexes*, 1927). Sechenov's idea was that even the most complex manifestations of human psychology were made up of reflexes, that is of ways of reacting to stimulation of the sensory nerves by specific muscular or glandular activities. This gave Pavlov encouragement to build up from his rigorous experiments on digestive reflexes a theory which he applied to all cerebral functions.

Although Pavlov's work has been influential in a number of ways, the clearest contrast with Darwin is in his application of rigorous experimental method. Darwin had relied on anecdotal reports of casual and informal observations. For instance, he attributed abstract thought to dogs on the basis of a game he played with his pet terrier: Darwin would say 'Hi, hi, where is it?' in an eager tone, and the terrier would rush around, apparently hunting for something. 'Now do not these actions clearly show that she had in her mind a general idea or concept that some animal is to be discovered or hunted?' asked Darwin (1871/1901, p. 127). This is unsatisfactory because there are several other possibilities. The eagerness of Darwin's tone of voice may simply have excited the dog, since there were no experimental controls to show that saying 'Where am I?' or 'How are you?' to the terrier might not elicit an equal amount of rushing about.

Pavlov's observations were the opposite of casual. As a professional research scientist under three Tzars, and then both Lenin and Stalin, he was known for his emphasis on rigorous experimental method, and the physiological tradition in which he worked required reliable and repeatable experimental demonstrations. In much of the later work, scrupulous care was taken to avoid extraneous influences on psychological experiments by keeping the human experimenter separate from the experimental animal in a different room, and by going to such lengths as building the laboratories with double walls filled with sand to achieve sound insulation. What Pavlov discovered, in the course of his systematic study of digestion, is that glandular secretions, of gastric juices or of saliva, are controlled by 'psychic' or psychological factors, and not simply by chemical or mechanical stimulation. The earliest way in which this was demonstrated was by 'sham feeding'.

It was primarily his skill as an experimental surgeon which enabled Pavlov to make his Nobel-prize-winning discoveries. Others, in the 1840s, had developed the technique of permanently implanting a metal tube in a dog's stomach, through which gastric juices could be collected. The modification introduced by Pavlov (and his co-worker, a Mrs Shumov-Simanovsky) was the surgical separation of the mouth from the stomach: the oesophagus was cut and the two cut ends were independently brought out at the throat. This meant that food eaten and swallowed by the dog dropped out of its throat before reaching the stomach, or alternatively, food could be dropped directly into the stomach without the dog's having seen or tasted it. The original purpose of this was to solve the problem of obtaining pure gastric juices, uncontaminated with food.

But, by the time of his Nobel lecture in 1904, Pavlov's main interest was in the psychological control of the gastric secretion. Bread dropped into a dog's stomach without the animal noticing it was not digested at all, but if the dog ate bread, gastric activity occurred even if the bread never reached the stomach. This all depended on the 'appetite' of the dog, since the mere sight of food produced stomach activity, but only if the dog took an interest in the food – the effectiveness of food in the mouth depends on how far the food 'suits the dog's taste' (Pavlov, 1955, p. 142).

In order to study these psychological factors in more detail it was not necessary to continue to work with secretions of the stomach, since secretions of the salivary glands can serve just as well. As every student knows, the standard Pavlovian experiment requires the measurement of salivation in response to an external and distant stimulus, such as the sounding of a buzzer. Dogs do not normally salivate when they hear buzzers, even if they are hungry, but, if the buzzer is always sounded a few seconds before food is to be presented, a 'conditioned reflex', of salivating to the sound, is formed. To establish a reliable response, a dog might be given half-a-dozen pieces of meat, each preceded by the sounding of the buzzer, at five-minute intervals every day for a week or more. After this, a demonstration of the 'conditioned reflex' could be given by simply sounding the buzzer, without giving any meat. Now the buzzer would produce the same effects, more or less, as showing the dog real food – there would be plenty of salivation, and the dog would lick its lips, look at the food dispenser and perhaps wag its tail.

More details of Pavlov's experimental findings will be found in chapter 3. The laboratory findings with the reflex of salivation were used as the basis for a theory about the 'higher nervous activity' of the mammalian cerebral hemispheres, and then for wide-ranging speculations about psychology and psychiatry. The dog salivates to the buzzer only because of its previous experience of the association in time of the buzzer with its food. The conditioned reflex could thus be seen as an atomic unit of learning from experience, capable of being 'synthesized' into more complex combinations by the activities of the cerebral cortex. Thus Pavlov was led to claim that 'the different kinds of habits based on training, education and discipline of any sort are *nothing but* a long chain of conditioned reflexes' (Pavlov, 1927, p. 295, my italics).

In some ways this set the pattern for subsequent learning theorists. In the last two pages of his *Conditioned Reflexes*, the most systematic exposition of his work, Pavlov reiterates his objective of providing a 'purely physiological interpretation' of brain activity immediately after asserting that his experiments would eventually 'throw some light upon one of the darkest points of our subjective self – namely, the relations between the conscious and the unconscious' (Pavlov, 1927, p. 410). Obviously, this harks back to Sechenov's slogan that 'all acts of conscious or unconscious life are reflexes', but, sadly, relations between conscious and unconscious processes are usually neglected in developments based on Pavlov's work.

Thorndike (1874–1949): connectionism and the law of effect

Pavlov often described stimuli such as the buzzer, which came to elicit salivation, as 'signals' for food, which might direct the animal to acquire food, and assist in its adaptation to the external world. But partly because in his experiments the dogs were firmly strapped in stands, he saw the formation of conditioned reflexes as a rather passive and mechanical process. Thorndike is important in learning theory for proposing an equally mechanical process of learning, but also for emphasizing the effects of consequences of the active response of an experimental animal. We may note, however, that Pavlov was not unaware of the influences of the consequences of an animal's actions, and made a special point in 1895 of mentioning an anecdote to illustrate this. Pavlov's most famous operation was the construction of 'Pavlov's pouch' (Gray, 1979) – a piece of the duodenum containing the outlet of the pancreas is cut away and then stitched back facing outwards so that it discharges through an opening in the abdomen, and its secretions can be subsequently collected. A difficulty with this was that the escaping digestive juices, leaking out during the night, caused erosion and bleeding of skin of the abdomen. One of the dogs subjected to his operation and left tied up in the laboratory overnight was found, two nights in succession, to have torn a heap of plaster from the wall. On the second occasion Pavlov noticed that the dog had been sleeping on the plaster, with the result that the skin of its abdomen was in exceptionally good condition. From then on all the animals that had had a similar operation were provided with a pile of sand or old mortar to lie on, which greatly reduced the incidence of skin irritations. Pavlov remarks: 'We gratefully acknowledge that by its manifestation of common sense the dog had helped us as well as itself. It would be a pity if this fact were lost for the psychology of the animal world' (Pavlov, 1955, p. 90).

Thorndike (1898) ensured that the tendency of animals to learn to help themselves was not lost to learning theory, but was reluctant to acknowledge anything approaching common sense on the part of the dogs, cats and chicks which were the subjects of his behavioural experiments. Whereas Pavlov brought to animal psychology a fully equipped physiological laboratory, Thorndike was influenced by the philosophical views of William James and by the fact that as a postgraduate student at Harvard in the 1890s he could conduct animal experiments only by keeping chickens, young cats and dogs in his own lodgings, and building his own apparatus. Not surprisingly, Thorndike was unpopular with landladies, and at one point, when Thorndike had been turned out for hatching chickens in his bedroom, William James's household had to take in both Thorndike and chickens. James's *Principles of Psychology* (1891) pours considerable scorn over Darwin's and Romanes' anecdotal evidence of reasoning in animals, and proposes that all their associations of ideas take place by simple contiguity. When an animal reacts intelligently to some stimulus, it is because 'the beast *feels like* acting so when these stimuli are present, though conscious of no definite reason why' (James, 1891, p. 350). In particular, when any animal opens a door or gate by biting or manipulating a latch or handle, James suggests that this is likely to be 'a random trick, learned by habit' (James, 1891, p. 353). Thorndike's bedroom experiments were designed to support these views of William James, which in many ways represented a reaction against Darwinian anthropomorphism and a return to the sceptical view of animal reason put forward in the seventeenth century by the English philosopher John Locke.

The main technique which Thorndike used to provide experimental evidence in support of James's view involved the use of problem or puzzle boxes, with cats (the barking of dogs having caused excessive trouble with landladies). The boxes were small crates, hammered together from wooden slats, about 50 cm square and 30 cm high. Anyone who has ever put a cat in a carrying box will know that they do not always take kindly to it, and Thorndike's animals, although less than a year old, struggled violently when they were first confined in the crates. In case they were in need of any further motivation to escape from the problem boxes, they were tested in a state described as 'utter hunger', with a piece of fish visible to them outside. In order for them to make their escape, it was necessary for them to find a releasing device which, when manipulated, would automatically allow a door to spring open. Several boxes were used, and for each one Thorndike had designed an ingenious arrangement of strings, pulleys and catches, which even the human observer would find hard to follow at first sight. Thus, when a cat was first put in one of the problem boxes, it did not sit back and deduce from the arrangement of pulleys which loop of string or catch had to be pulled, but rather scratched and cried, and thrust its paws or nose into any available opening, until by chance it made some movement which operated the release mechanism. On average, with one of the simpler boxes, it would take a cat five minutes of random scratching before it accidentally succeeded on the first test, but after ten or twenty trials in the same box it would consistently escape within five seconds or so (see figure 3, p. 48).

Thorndike attributed this change in behaviour to random, or 'trial-and-error', learning. The form which the learning took (Thorndike's answer to the question 'What is learned?) he supposed to be a 'connection between the situation and a certain impulse to act' which is 'stamped in when pleasure results from the act, and stamped out when it doesn't' (Thorndike, 1898, p. 103). Thorndike called himself a connectionist, and it was connections between stimulus input and response output which were learned, whether one thinks in terms of connections between perceptions and impulses to act or in terms of connections between neurons in the brain.

There are two things to notice about Thorndike's explanation. First, it is a pleasure/pain, or reward and punishment, theory. It is because the cat is glad, or satisfied, when it gets out of the box, that it learns the trick. Secondly, and this is an odd thing about Thorndike's theory, the cat is not supposed to think ahead about getting out – it has an impulse to perform the releasing action, but no anticipation that the action will lead to its release. This sounds rather unlikely, as far as the cat experiment goes, but it followed on from William James's views, and as a simple generalization the 'law of effect' proved to be a very powerful assumption. The law of effect is the statement that the effects of an action (whether it produces reward or punishment) act backwards to stamp in the connection between the action and the circumstances in which it was made. Although more recent authorities would suggest that Thorndike's cats operated the catches and pulled strings in their boxes because they expected to get out by these means, there are other cases where the backwards-stamping-in aspect of rewards is significant, and the idea that responses can be changed by their consequences has an important place in learning theory.

Watson (1878–1958) and behaviourism

The idea that an animal's pleasure or discomfort could encourage it to repeat, or abstain from, actions which brought about such states did not at first form part of Watson's behaviourism. It was listed under 'certain misconceptions' in Watson's book of 1914, where he said that 'It is our aim to combat the idea that pleasure or pain has anything to do with habit formation' (p. 257). Having devoted, by 1913, twelve years to studying animal behaviour, in the laboratory and in the field, Watson had become impatient with the difficulties of integrating his findings with the contemporary psychology based on human introspection, and attempted to throw out all talk of feelings, conscious sensations and images from psychological discussion, hoping to produce 'a purely objective experimental branch of natural science'. This approach certainly made it easier to be systematic about such things as colour vision in animals. If a bird is exposed to red and green lights, it will never be possible to decide whether the animal subjectively sees the two colours in the same way as I do, or sees them as two shades of grey, or as anything else. But it is relatively easy to do an experiment to train the bird to respond to the red light and not to the green one, and then to make variations in the lights to find out the relative importance of the brightness and wavelength of the light as influences on the animal's behaviour.

However, Watson's behaviourism also led him to say things he later regretted, such as 'thought processes are really motor habits in the larynx' (1913, p. 174). By 1931, this extreme view had been altered slightly: 'I have tried everywhere to emphasize the enormous complexity of the musculature in the throat and chest. . . . the muscular habits learned in overt speech are responsible for implicit or internal speech (thought)' (Watson, 1931, pp. 238–9).

The title of the book from which these quotations are taken is *Behaviorism*, and the extract makes it quite clear that Watson wished to interpret all mental activity in terms of peripheral movements and habits of movement – this is a defining feature of behaviourism, but not of all learning theories, as we shall see.

Like most learning theorists, Watson discussed human behaviour in terms of motives and rewards. A dress designer creates a new gown, he says, not by having 'pictures in his mind', but by calling a model in, throwing a piece of material around her, and manipulating it until his own emotional reactions are aroused in a satisfactory way and the assistants say 'Magnifique!' (1931, p. 248). This of course is trial and error, or 'trial and success', as Thorndike often called it.

Watson did his Ph.D. thesis on animal learning a couple of years after Thorndike, and published it as *Animal Education* (1903). The experiments involved problem boxes and mazes which hungry animals learned to get out of for food rewards, and differed from Thorndike's mainly in that the subjects were white rats instead of chickens and cats. But Watson resisted Thorndike's idea that rewards 'stamped in' responses, and preferred to talk simply of the formation or fixation of habits. Animals learned how to get out of problem boxes, according to Watson, partly because the response they happened to make just before leaving the box had to be the last one in a series of responses to the same stimulus – the recency effect. In time, the correct solution to a problem becomes the most frequent response, and Watson left it at that. The frequency principle, especially when rendered as the importance of practice and repetition, is common to many other theorists, notably Guthrie (1886–1959).

As a propagandist, Watson was fond of going to extremes, and one can be most sympathetic to him in this when he argues against racial and familial inferiority. Since Watson was brought up as a poor white in South Carolina, he knew well enough the strength of the opposition to his view that neither Negroes in general nor distinguished white families in particular had inherited tendencies and psychological factors to thank for their social position. It is 'millions of conditionings' during early childhood experience in upbringing and education that are responsible, in Watson's theories, for both the personalities and the intellectual capacities of adults. His most famous assertion was:

> Give me a dozen healthy infants, well-formed, and my own specified world to bring them up in and I'll guarantee to take any one at random and train him to become any type of specialist I might select – doctor, lawyer, artist, merchant-chief, and, yes, even beggar-man and thief, regardless of his talents, penchants, tendencies, abilities, vocations, and race of his ancestors. (Watson, 1931, p. 104)

This is certainly a strong claim for the importance of learning in human psychology.

Skinner (1904–) and operant conditioning

B.F. Skinner belongs to a much later academic generation than Thorndike and Watson, but he can be regarded as having amalgamated these two earlier theorists into a new blend which has outlasted the original components. Thorndike's experiments on the law of effect have priority as the first investigations of operant conditioning, as Skinner acknowledges, but the Watsonian emphasis on habits and reflexes, and the popularity of behaviourism, left Thorndike isolated. While believing in associations and connections, Thorndike was always closer to William James than to Watson. Thorndike's *Elements of Psychology* (1905) is almost entirely concerned with mental states and feelings – these two terms being used in most of the chapter headings, as in 'Feelings of things as absent: images and memories' and 'Mental states concerned in the directions of conduct: feelings of willing'. In the year that Watson began his crusade for behaviourism, Thorndike was still introducing the law of effect in a chapter on 'Consciousness, learning and remembering'. It was left to Skinner to bring the trial-and-success principle into the Watsonian world of reflexes.

This happened fairly gradually. Skinner's first work (1931) was a behaviourist analysis of the concept of the reflex, in Pavlov's experiments and those of other physiologists, and the results of experiments on rats in the famous 'Skinner box' were reported as experiments on reflexes. But in a series of papers Skinner drove a wedge between reflexes of the Pavlovian type (eventually terming these 'respondents') and habits of the Thorndikean kind (eventually calling these 'operants'). In these early papers, Skinner was fond of drawing diagrams to show the sequences of stimulus and response in conditioning. Thus $S_0 - R_0$; $S_1 - R_1$ described what happened in the first Skinner boxes. These contained an automatic dispenser to drop small pellets of food, one at a time, into a food tray, and just above the food tray a horizontal wire lever, which, when pushed down by the rat, could operate the automatic dispenser. In the sequence of Ss and Rs, $S_0 - R_0$ would be the stimulus of the sight or the touch of the lever leading to the response of the rats of pressing it down, and $S_1 - R_1$ would be the consequent stimulus of a food pellet dropping into the tray, and the response of the rat of seizing and eating the food pellet. Clearly the description could be broken down further (including even the swallowing reflexes of the animal), but Skinner's point was that there was a 'chain' of responses, and the 'getting-the-food part' of the chain strengthened the 'pressing-the-lever part' which preceded it, the 'strengthening' being a more neutral and purely descriptive version of Thorndike's 'stamping in' (see Skinner, 1938, pp. 47–54, 65–6).

By 1938, Skinner emphasized that in 'operant' behaviour – moving about in the environment and manipulating things – there is no static connection of a response with a previous eliciting stimulus, but rather a response is 'emitted' in a more or less spontaneous and voluntary way. This may be contrasted with a knee-jerk or finger-from-flame withdrawal, which is always related to the eliciting stimulus. Sometimes these distinctions become very technical. But a 'reflex of seeking food' (Skinner, 1935, p. 176) as active, goal-determined responding is clearly rather different from the secretion of saliva and gastric juices of a dog strapped in a stand in Pavlov's experiments, and more like intentional trial and error.

Although operant goal seeking sounds slightly mentalistic, Skinner exceeded even Watson's rigour in sustained scepticism about inner mental images and desires. Operant responses were not supposed to be chained together because they made up purposeful acts, but only because, in echoes of Thorndike, 'The connections between parts are purely mechanical' (1938, p. 55). Inner mental events, Skinner usually supposes, are no more necessary as explanations of operant behaviour than they are for the sequences of reflexes used in swallowing or the maintenance of postures (1938, p. 54, 1977). But he has been able to say provocative things about private stimuli and functional units in thinking and speaking, in very much the same way as Watson was able to talk about 'language habits'. The most theoretical part of Skinner's work is his claim to have no theory at all (1950) and to be a radical behaviourist who simply describes the facts and nothing but the facts.

Hull (1884–1952) and mathematical equations in learning theory

In the 1930s, while Skinner was working out that Thorndike's results were different from Pavlov's, C.L. Hull, at Yale, was saying that they boiled down to the same thing. Hull's theories were extremely influential during his lifetime, but after his death, Skinner, who had returned to Harvard from Indiana in 1948, became the most notable figure concerned with animal learning.

Hull's theory was extremely systematic, and could often be stated in mathematical equations; these made it easier to show that the theory was, in most significant respects, wrong. It was most famously and instructively wrong over the question of needs, drives and incentives. Hull's theory has been called 'hypothetico-deductive' because he believed in starting from first principles, and setting down postulates and corollaries in mathematical or logical forms. But Darwinian first principles led him astray almost immediately. 'Animals may almost be regarded as aggregations of needs' (1943, p. 64) is true enough, but Hull took the idea too far. In Thorndike's cat-in-the-box experiment it seems reasonable to say that the cat, if hungry, has a need for the food outside, and that, if it struggles, it appears to have a drive to escape, as well as a 'hunger drive'. Hull went on from this to formulate various elaborations of the law of effect in terms of need reduction. Postulate III (1952) runs:

> Whenever an effector activity is closely associated with a stimulus afferent impulse or trace and the conjunction is closely associated with a rapid diminution in the motivational stimulus there will result an increment to a tendency for that stimulus to evoke that response. (p. 5)

This is very close to Thorndike's idea of the stamping-in of connections by pleasurable consequences, but here it is a reduction of a drive which increases the likelihood of a future response to the stimulus. It was the essence of Hull's system that he did not add qualifications such as 'other things being equal' or 'depending on whether the animal is paying attention to what it is doing', as Thorndike did – animals were supposed to *always* learn response tendencies under appropriate conditions of drive reduction, and *never* learn anything if there was not any drive reduction. Tolman and others (see pp. 16ff.) provided evidence to show that rats apparently learned a good deal without any obvious drive reduction, and that learning does not only take the form of tendencies for stimuli to elicit responses, and Hull's theory became more and more complicated and cumbersome. After various articles, the first in 1929, the 1936 presidential address to the American Psychological Association (1937) and the book *Principles of Behavior* (1943), Hull's final system (1952) needed thirty-two separate postulates. The main one of general application was this:

$$_{S}E_{R} = D \times V \times K \times {_{S}H_{R}}$$

This implies that the intensity or likelihood of any learned behaviour ($_{S}E_{R}$) can be calculated if four other factors are known – the drive or motivation associated with it (D); the intensity of the signal for the behaviour (V); the degree of incentive (K); and the level of habit ($_{S}H_{R}$). Under laboratory conditions all the factors can be measured, and the equation checked. $_{S}E_{R}$ is measured by the probability or strength of a response, D by hours of deprivation or some other indicator of physical need, K by the size of the reward or some other index of its desirability, and $_{S}H_{R}$ is calculated as the amount of practice given – usually as a number of reinforcements, each episode of drive reduction being one reinforcement.

The gradual increase in response tendency or habit with repeated experience is the core of the Hullian system, and the mathematical treatment of gradually changing associations is a bit of flotsam remaining from its wreckage. When a response tendency increases, in Hull's system, *the increase equals a fraction of (the maximum of the habit minus its current level)*. This always gives a nice gentle approach to the final level of habit (or asymptote). If the final level is taken as 100 units, and the fraction as a tenth (Hull, 1943, p. 115), then on the first learning trial the increase will be 10 units; but by the time the habit is half formed at 50 units, which takes 7 trials, the increase is down to 5 units (1/10 (100–50)), and by the time the response tendency is 90 per cent complete (after 22 trials) each increment is of course less than 1. The closer to the maximum, the smaller the increments get.

This started as a matter of algebraic convenience, but by a quirk of fate 'a modification of Hull's account of the growth of $_{S}H_{R}$', proposed long after his death by two of his successors at Yale (Rescorla and Wagner, 1972, p. 75), has proved to be surprisingly popular (Dickinson, 1980; Hilgard and Bower, 1981). Rescorla and Wagner were concerned with experiments of a Pavlovian kind, where two stimuli are given at once. As an example we may consider a Pavlovian dog whose food is signalled by both a buzzer and a flashing light – how much would it salivate to the light or buzzer presented alone? Hull's algebra can be modified to treat separately the tendency of each stimulus to elicit salivation, by saying that whenever there is an increase for an individual stimulus *the increase equals a fraction of (the maximum response minus the current tendency of both stimuli)*. This deals quite well with cases such as that where the dog has already been conditioned to salivate to the buzzer before a flashing light is made to accompany the buzzer. If the buzzer was already firmly conditioned, and close to the maximum by itself, the equation says there can be very little increase in the tendency to salivate to the light, and indeed, in this sort of experiment, the dog would probably ignore it.

Tolman's ideas and expectancies

When Rescorla and Wagner (1972) presented their rather Hullian model for findings in classical conditioning, they made a prefatory comment that an alternative version of the model would be expressed by saying 'organisms only learn when events violate their expectations' (p. 75). If a dog has already learned to expect food when it hears a buzzer, adding a flashing lamp along with the buzzer is redundant, and the dog will not pay it much attention. It is now fairly common for theories about animal learning to be presented in terms of expectations, or 'expectancies' (Mackintosh, 1974; Walker, 1983), and this is something which goes back to Tolman. The terminology is indicative of a larger theoretical debt.

Starting with 'A new formula for behaviorism' (1922), Tolman always called himself a behaviourist, but disowned Watsonian 'muscle twitchism', and recommended that objective measurements of behaviour should be used to support 'molar' concepts or 'intervening variables'. During his career Tolman used rather a wide variety of terms to describe these concepts, including 'beliefs', 'hypotheses' and 'representations', as well as the more obscure 'sign-Gestalt' and 'means-ends readiness', and the now familiar 'cognitive map' (Tolman, 1948). But his theoretical position is most clearly set out in the early papers in which he proposed that animal learning is determined by 'purpose and cognition' (1925), and that because of this it is possible to have 'a behavioristic theory of ideas' (1926). In animal experiments, we can observe 'in-behaviour' ideas, because behaviour may be caused by purposes – 'purposes which exhibit themselves as persistences through trial and error to get to or from', and may express cognitions – 'cognitions as to the nature of the environment for mediating such gettings to or from' (1951, p. 51). The behavioural evidence from the kittens getting out of Thorndike's puzzle box suggested to Tolman that the animals had rather simple ideas – 'getting out of the box' was related to 'eating the food', and also 'clawing at the loop' was related to 'getting out of the box' – without mechanical insight into the relation between the loop of string and the door. He thought that the cat had only 'a representation of the very immediate consequences of the act, a prevision, perhaps of the opening of the door' (1951, pp. 58, 60). Nowadays, it is often inferred that animals may have inner representations of future events, as in a 'unitary representation' of two stimuli presented together, or in 'multiple representations' of the same stimulus or in 'reinforcer-specific expectancies', the inferences being made from an examination of detailed experimental evidence. Tolman's own preferred form of experiment was the study of maze-learning in rats – in his view the best way to examine ideas was not to introspect on one's own but to look at 'a really good rat in a really good maze' (see Tolman's *Collected Papers*, 1951, p. 62). Mazes often demonstrate something which we ought anyway to expect on the basis of an animal's natural life – that most species can acquire a knowledge of local geography which is not coded as sequences of muscle movements. There is still a good deal of uncertainty about exactly how homing pigeons get home, but they definitely do not do it only because of a collection of wing-flapping tendencies:

visual landmarks are important, at least at close range. In the case of rats in mazes, experiments in Tolman's laboratory showed that a rat who has learned the maze by running can successfully swim round the maze when it is flooded (and vice versa); this shows it is not the individual movements of walking or swimming that constitute the learning of the maze. Various experiments on 'place-learning' demonstrate that organized information about the spatial layout of mazes is available to rats, enabling them to make shortcuts or go in the correct direction towards the usual location of food from several different starting points, and this is evidence for 'cognitive maps' rather than habit sequences.

So far, this means that Tolman's answer to the question 'What is learned?' is much more complicated than stimulus-response connections or response tendencies. But it does not bear on the questions 'How is it learned? or 'When is it learned?', which were both answered by the law of effect or the drive-reduction postulate in the theories of Thorndike and Hull.

Latent learning Maze experiments by Tolman and Honzik (1930) showed that learning could take place without any drive reduction, or stamping-in of connections by pleasure or pain. Rats were run on 'multiple T' mazes (see figure 1) in which the correct way through involved a sequence of fourteen choices (to turn left or right) in correct order. Hungry rats given some food at the end of the maze once a day seemed gradually to learn the correct sequence, taking up to two weeks to reduce their mistakes (turning into blind alleys) to a minimum. This could be taken to mean that correct turning habits were being stamped in by the rewards, since animals not given any food at the end hardly reduced their mistakes at all. But, if the rats who had been through the mazes without any food for ten days (being fed in their home cages) suddenly found some food at the end of it, then, on the next day, they ran through almost perfectly. The obvious interpretation is that they had learned a cognitive map of how to get through the maze during the first ten days, but had not bothered to take the quickest route – hence the learning was 'latent', or 'behaviourally silent'. But, once they discovered food at the end – even after an incorrect run – then, on the next day, the expectation that food might be available again was sufficient motivation for them to manifest their previous learning by running the maze correctly

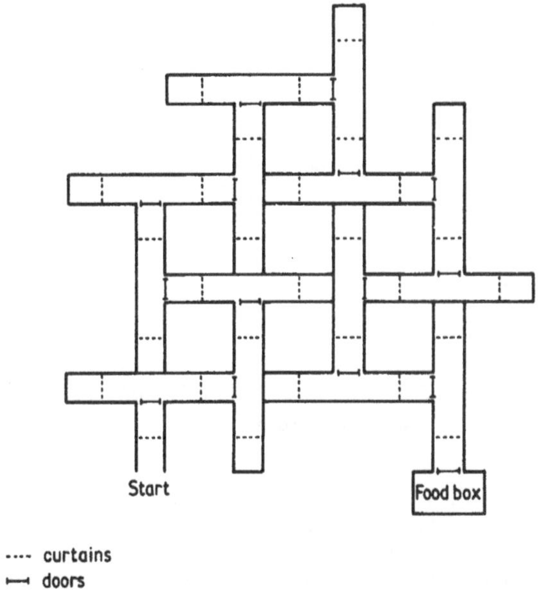

Figure 1 A fourteen-turn maze used by Tolman.
This was the kind of maze used in the first studies of 'latent learning'. To run through it without any errors, rats have to make fourteen turns in the sequence r, l, l, r, r, l, r, r, l, r, r, l, l, r. The alleys are four or five inches wide, with high walls and a system of curtains and doors which prevents the animals from seeing the next clear turn, but does not prevent them using more remote visual cues such as light sources. (After Tolman, 1948)

(figure 2). Clearly, the motivation, and the food, are important influences on the rats' behaviour, or on their performance, but the acquisition of spatial knowledge can go on quite well in the absence of any obvious drive reduction, or external reward.

Summary

A discussion of how learning from experience has been incorporated into psychological theories could be widened to include a great deal more material than I have covered in this brief and selective review. Darwinian evolution suggested that there must

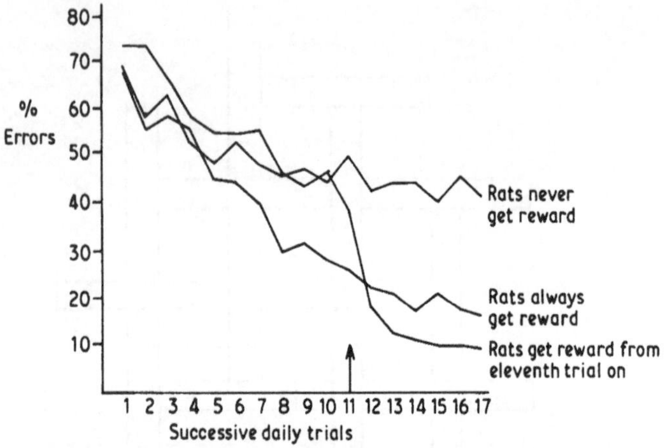

Figure 2 Latent learning results.
The obvious way of getting a rat to learn a maze is to provide it with a food incentive at the end. Rats always rewarded in this way show a gradual decrease in errors (turning the wrong way in a maze like that shown in figure 1). Rats who are never rewarded continue to make many errors. But animals run initially without any food incentive (in this case for the first ten days), who have apparently learned nothing, show an immediate improvement in performance after just one reward, proving that some learning had taken place on the non-rewarded trials, even though this was not obvious in the rats' behaviour until rewards were given. (After Tolman and Honzik, 1930)

be a gradual development of psychological capacities, from species to species, and this gave a boost to all studies of animal behaviour. But the learning theories developed from the results of Pavlov's experiments on conditioned reflexes and Thorndike's experiments on trial-and-error learning are notable because of the search for general laws of learning. First Watson, and then Skinner, emphasized overt and directly measurable behaviour, learned as habits and reflexes. Skinner has followed Thorndike in pointing to external reinforcements consisting of reward and punishment as the primary causes of trial-and-error learning, or operant conditioning, while Hull maintained for some time that internal drive reduction was the reinforcement for trial-and-error learning and Pavlov's classical conditioning alike.

Much current work follows Tolman in deducing that learning can occur without any reward and indeed without any immediate effects on behaviour. These are all differences between learning theories, but they have much in common, and some of the common factors will be examined in the next chapter.

2

Common factors in learning theories

There is today no shortage of dispute among those working in the fields of learning theory and behaviour modification. New experimental techniques, and new theoretical attacks on old problems mean that any overview is likely to be temporary. But it is possible to draw out some themes from previous work, at least from the selection of theories examined in the last chapter, before going on to look at particular experimental questions.

Species differences

First of all, of course, it is obvious that the theories are about animal learning, or are theories which are being tested in animal experiments. We shall see later that this does not imply a lack of concern with the human condition altogether. Also, the theories are attempts to discover principles about animals in general, even though evidence from only a few species is quoted and most of the data concern laboratory rats. All the theories are open to criticism on this account – there may be enormous differences between species (and especially differences between the human species and all others) which mean that the search for general principles will always end in disillusion. Martin Seligman (1970), for instance, argued that there could be no general laws of learning; but subsequently has been concerned to establish a very general theory about the cause and cure of human depression, based on laboratory experiments with dogs (Seligman, 1975).

Clearly, learning theories are based on the assumption that there is some discoverable logic to behaviour, over and above the biological details of species differences. This assumption is older than Darwin and in some senses theories about learning from experience are more philosophical than biological. Ideas in learning theory, like ideas in just about everything else, go back to Aristotle, and the first case in point is the concern with generalizations over and above species differences. To introduce *De motu animalium*, Aristotle says:

> The movements of the animals that belong to each genus, and how these are differentiated, and what the reasons are for the particular characters of each – all this we have considered elsewhere. But now we must consider in general the common reason for moving with any movement whatever. (from Nussbaum, 1978)

Translating movement into behaviour, this would serve to introduce almost any learning theory, since it is common reasons, and general principles, that are almost always being sought. The particular theory which Aristotle introduces is not unlike Tolman's: movement in animals arises when 'the painful is avoided and the pleasant pursued' (from Nussbaum, 1978, p. 44), but in general 'the movers of the animal are reasoning and imagination and choice and wish and appetite. And all of these can be reduced to thought and desire' (from Nussbaum, 1978, p. 38). For Aristotle thought and desire are apparent in movement from place to place, just as purpose and cognition are revealed, according to Tolman, in maze-learning, and in this case differences between the human species and others are often ignored.

As I write this on his eightieth birthday, I am prompted to acknowledge that Sir Karl Popper, the distinguished philosopher and in some ways the Aristotle of today, is also someone who has tried hard to establish logical principles of behaviour that transcend species differences. Sir Karl is very fond of provocatively comparing Einstein with the amoeba: 'from the amoeba to Einstein is just one step'. This is because of a philosophical theory about the growth of knowledge with learning from experience: 'From the amoeba to Einstein, the growth of knowledge is always the same'. It is the same because, according to Popper 'All *organisms* are constantly, day and night, *engaged in problem solving*', and 'Problem solving always proceeds by the method of trial and error' (Popper, 1972, pp. 246, 261, 242 respectively; see Magee, 1975, pp. 56–73). This is a rather special sort of theory, which attempts to interpret many different kinds of things as a sequence of variation and selective retention, rather as in Darwinian evolution. But it contains strange echoes of the cats' trial-and-error solutions in Thorndike's problem boxes, and Watson also used the device of saying 'No new principle is needed in passing from the unicellular organisms to man' (Watson, 1914, p. 318).

This is not the place to disagree with Popper, or even with Watson – I am quoting the 'amoeba to Einstein' comparison to suggest that from Watson to Popper is just one step, and that it may sometimes be respectable to put species differences to one side. But it must be said that the learning abilities of amoeba tend to be vastly overrated. Both Watson and Popper had read the work of Herbert Spencer Jennings, who assumed that if only amoebae were the size of dogs we would assess amoeba intelligence as just like the dog's (Jennings, 1906, p. 336). This is utter nonsense (Bovee and Lahn, 1973). Not only is it absurd to think of amoebae playfully fetching sticks, or obeying their master's voice, there is not a scrap of decent evidence to suggest that amoebae have any kind of conditioned reflexes, let alone trial-and-error learning. Some amoebae move around a lot, and will slide around inedible obstacles, and engulf and consume palatable ones (some amoebae being ecologically classified as 'carnivorous predators'). To this extent they are solving objective problems of life, and they are certainly exhibiting a variety of objectively classifiable behaviours: they share both these features with Einstein. But if it is only one step between the amoeba and Einstein, it is a step with a very large number of stages, of which the most significant are having a nervous system – of even the jellyfish type; having a brain and spinal cord; being a mammal; being a person; and last, but not least, knowing some physics.

It is usually a flaw in learning theories that, even if these big stages are acknowledged, some of the smaller ones, such as the gaps between rat and monkey, and monkey and man, are not; but it is probably necessary to stand well back from species differences in order to distinguish the wood from the trees, and to claim general principles and universal laws. A biological approach to the study of behaviour which is perhaps more realistic can be found in Lea (1984; see also Walker, 1983).

Once one suspends belief in species differences, then any codification of learning from experience could be called general. But although there are as many learning theories as there are theorists, there is always some attempt to narrow down, and specify, basic processes in terms of which a wide range of possibilities can be understood. Either the exterior conditions under which learning may or may not be supposed to occur are specified, or alternatively an attempt may be made to specify internal theoretical mechanisms.

Association by contiguity in time

It is sometimes said that the first learning theorists were 'British empiricist' philosophers, who stressed that sense experience, plus subsequent mental operations, determined human thought. The association of ideas due to contiguity in time was introduced by Locke (1632–1704), who was English, as an afterthought to explain irrational connections of ideas, such as aversions to foods whose ingestion has only accidentally preceded illness, or a dislike of books resulting from painful experiences at school. Berkeley (1685–1753), who was Irish, said that it was only because initially arbitrary visual experiences are observed 'constantly to go together' with tangible ideas of size and distance, as when we actually walk towards someone else and touch them, that we can have visual ideas of size and distance. Hume (1711–76), who was Scottish, said that all inferences from experience are based on custom, or habit; that custom is the 'great guide of human life'; and that exactly the same principles determine cognition in people as in animals. Hume then obviously has a claim to be the first learning theorist, and, according to the recent biography (Cohen, 1979), he was a direct influence on J.B. Watson, who was exhilarated and liberated by his first reading of Hume, and read him again while running his first experiments. Hume mentioned both the mere contiguity of events, and the special case of reward and punishment:

> animals and men learn many things from experience, and infer, that the same events will always follow from the same causes. By this principle they become acquainted with the more obvious properties of external objects. . . . This is still more obvious from the effects of discipline and education on animals, who, by the proper application of rewards and punishments, may be taught any course of action, and most contrary to their natural instincts and propensities. (Hume, 1777/1970, p. 105)

The principle of association of ideas by the contiguity of events in time was incorporated into many philosophical systems until the nineteenth century. The most important is the system of Herbert Spencer since he combined the principle of association with a general theory of evolution (his term, not Darwin's) and a concept of reflex action, which guided the theories of Pavlov (1927, p. 9) and Maudsley (see chapter 9). Spencer's two-volume *Principles of Psychology* (1855) is based on association by contiguity, which he supposes to be due to the results of waves of activity passing through the nervous system:

> Hence the growth of intelligence at large depends on the law, that when any two psychical states occur in immediate succession, an effect is produced such that if the first subsequently recurs there is a certain tendency for the second to follow it. . . . By this law, if it is the true one, must be interpretable all the phenomena, from the lowest to the highest. (Spencer, 1855/1899, p. 425)

If there is a single feature common to all learning theories, it is the principle that, when one thing follows another in the experience of an individual animal or person, something happens, so that those two things become in some way more associated than they were before. Exactly what has to follow what, and exactly what happens then that produces the observed increase in association between these two units, are of course matters of some dispute. The associated things in the original theories were always mental impressions or ideas, and currently a similar level of association would be said to exist between 'central representations'. But those interested in underlying mechanisms have been inclined to assume that waves of activity in the cerebral cortex, or the firing tendencies of individual neurons, must be the physiological causes of psychological effects. And perhaps the most notable aspect of the twentieth-century, and mainly American, interpretation of associations is an insistence that behavioural description is more important than hypothetical neurological changes, or unmeasureable subjective impressions. The typical behaviourist, such as Watson or Skinner, resents the nervous system just as much as he resents subjective ideas, if not more so, since neural events are remote from the here-and-now physical interaction of the whole animal with the world.

Whatever the things associated, whether mental ideas or behaviourally defined stimuli and responses, there are a number of possible forms that associations might take. The most notable tradition in learning theory has been to restrict associations to modifications of the input–output rebound effect which is inherent in the physiological concept of a reflex. Thus Thorndike's connections were between sensory feelings and impulses to respond, and many subsequent writers supposed that learning consists mainly in alterations to stimulus-response connections, or S-R bonds. There are other possible forms of association, of course, and some of these others have current interest. Mackintosh (1974) interprets the results of trial-and-error learning in terms of associations between responses and their consequences, which would be response-stimulus or 'R-S' connections. Thus, according to this view, in Thorndike's experiment the cat learns an association between the response of pressing a latch, and the stimulus of getting out and eating fish. On the other hand Mackintosh suggests that in Pavlovian experiments an association is commonly formed between two stimuli (giving an 'S-S' connection) – for instance when the dog forms an association between the stimulus of hearing the buzzer and the stimulus of tasting the meat.

These last examples point to the role of purpose or desire in the process of learning, or, to use more objective terms, to the role of drive conditions and motivating stimuli. Thorndike assumed that motivating stimuli were essential for any trial-and-error learning to take place: if one were not dissatisfied with error, or satisfied with success, then there would be no mechanism of selecting one response over another, and changing behaviour. However, since Tolman's experiments, it has become necessary to distinguish between *learning* and *performance* – it is assumed that rats can learn the way through a maze with no reward, but will only actually perform the learned act, that is run through the maze correctly, when there is a goal of food at the end. For many practical purposes, it is performance that counts, and therefore the goal, or the motivation, or the drive is paramount. But with the possible exception of Skinnerians who take into account only 'reinforcement', most theorists distinguish in some way between pure practice, or the acquisition of neutral information, on the one hand; and motivating conditions which may influence learning, and will certainly determine actual behaviour, on the other hand.

Even for highly charged behaviours, neutral information may be necessary. 'I have to drink' says thirst; 'Here's drink' says the cognitive map. The cognitive map and the thirst are separate, because rats will learn where water is even when they are not thirsty (Spence and Lippsit, 1946).

Voluntary and involuntary behaviour

The effects of learning from experience and the effects of motivation have thus to be kept separate, even though it may be rare to find effects of one kind in the absence of those of the other. But motivation enters into another important distinction – between voluntary and involuntary behaviour. There is a sense in which Thorndike's cats were working out for themselves a solution to a problem, and were voluntarily learning to get out of the box in which they were confined. It is certainly arguable that, if a cat successfully scratches at the door to be let out, it is leaving the house of its own volition. By comparison, Pavlov's dogs, strapped in a stand, learned in a more passive way – there was no active responding necessary for them to try out, and the criterion of learning was that salivation, a glandular response which is surely involuntary, occurred when an external stimulus, the buzzer, was imposed on the animals. There is an input versus output distinction here as well; although standing and listening, or sitting and watching, may be voluntary and relatively passive, while running away, or panic-stricken struggling, may be involuntary and relatively active. Perceiving is in any case often regarded as active, involving attention and expectancies, whether voluntary or not, but I think it is still best to talk both about stimuli, as involving the sense organs, and responses, as requiring motor apparatus. Digging the garden uses up a lot more calories than watching television, and the amount of energy, or effort, or concentration that is used or needed in a given activity will usually have something to do with motivation.

There are in fact many tricky difficulties involved in making satisfactory distinctions between voluntary and involuntary responses, but running about and waving the forelimbs tend to be more readily put to the service of anticipated goals than, say, insomnia or nausea. Some of these difficulties will come up in later chapters. Perhaps the simplest distinction is that learning to be motivated may be different from motivated learning, that is, learning to want something, or learning to be afraid, differs from learning how to get what is wanted, or how to avoid what is feared.

Nurture versus nature in the control of behaviour

It would be possible to construct a pessimistic learning theory, which listed all the difficulties involved in ever learning anything, and specified the various conditions under which learning is extremely unlikely. But, as a matter of fact, most of the learning theorists so far mentioned have been great optimists. They believed in the first place that learning, according to the principles they laid down, was a widespread influence on behaviour throughout the animal kingdom; and in the second place that if only the same principles of learning were properly applied to human life, there would result vastly improved techniques of everything from child-rearing and sex education to the management of schizophrenia and industrial relations. Clearly, if general principles exist and we can discover the fundamental laws of a universal logic of behaviour, then there might be some benefits to be derived from applying them. Perhaps almost as important as the laws themselves is the optimism that there are new solutions to old problems. At any rate, as of now, there are numerous journals devoted to behaviour modification or behaviour therapy which, although they are proceeding under their own steam of practical usefulness, owe a great deal of their initial impetus to the theories discussed in this and the last chapter. I shall return to the question of how this came about in later chapters.

3

Pavlovian conditioning: reflexes, expectancies and involuntary emotional associations

The development of Pavlov's experimental method of producing conditioned salivation in dogs was described in chapter 1, and a discussion of Pavlov's application of his findings to the problems of human psychology will be found in chapter 6. Here I intend to give an up-to-date account of a selection of experiments and theories in the area, which has come to be known as classical conditioning.

The descriptive essence of classical conditioning is: first find a stimulus that reliably elicits a certain response from an animal (an unconditioned stimulus, UCS or US). Then we can take another stimulus, which initially does not elicit that response, and set up pairings of the two stimuli, in which the initially ineffective stimulus precedes the effective one. As a consequence, the original response comes to be given to a new stimulus. (The new stimulus is a 'conditioned stimulus', or CS, which elicits the conditioned response, CR, a version of the original unconditioned response, the UCR or UR.) Thus, in Pavlov's experiment, dogs which initially salivated when they saw food, but not when they heard buzzers, came to salivate when they heard buzzers after Pavlov, in a special experimental room, had made the buzzer sound as a signal for a few seconds before food was mechanically delivered. This may be called 'associative learning' because the response of salivation is now apparently associated with buzzers, whereas it was not to start with.

But, because many experiments, done with many species of animal, from tadpoles to tabby cats, can all be *described* as classical conditioning (since in all cases a response becomes associated with a new stimulus), it does not follow that there is a single mechanism, or a single psychological *explanation*, that applies equally to all cases, or to all species.

Pavlov subtitled his main book (1927) *An Investigation of the Physiological Activity of the Cerebral Cortex*, and its first sentence is: 'The cerebral hemispheres stand out as the crowning achievement in the nervous development of the animal kingdom.' He himself was aiming at a theory of the crowning achievement, not a reduction to a common factor of neural adaptability. Thus he ends his first chapter by saying that 'The essential feature of the highest activity of the central nervous system, with which we are concerned . . . consists not in the fact that innumerable signalling stimuli do initiate reactions in the animal, but in the fact that under different conditions these same stimuli may initiate quite different reactions' (1927, p. 14). It is flexibility, not knee-jerk-like predictability, which is the essential feature, and which demonstrates the 'analysing and synthesizing' functions of the mammalian brain. And partly because the brain is such a 'complex dynamic system', 'the method of conditioned reflexes will also have its limitations' (1927, p. 130).

Sadly, most of Pavlov's complex dynamics of analysis and synthesis were left out of learning theories like Watson's and Hull's, and there is still a tendency to assume that all classical conditioning is exactly the same, and is always an example of a single process of 'associative learning', which can be observed in even the simplest of organisms. For instance, a recent paper is titled 'Associative learning in *Aplysia*: evidence for conditioned fear in an invertebrate' (Walters *et al.*, 1981). Giving electric shocks to the head of a sea slug makes it withdraw its head (an unconditioned response), and if shrimp extract is squirted at its head several times a day a minute before shock is given, this makes the slug slightly more likely to withdraw its head when squirted with shrimp extract on subsequent tests. The authors simply state that 'associative learning occurs in gastropod molluscs' and, as these molluscs are also capable of swimming away from 'conditioned fear stimuli', they put forward the 'conditioned fear hypothesis'. I have not seen it yet, but I presume that even now work is under way which will be reported as 'experimental neurosis' and 'learned helplessness' in *Aplysia californica* (a sea slug).

Such work has many virtues, but among them is the fact that it points up the necessity of making theoretical distinctions between phenomena, all describable as classical conditioning, which occur under varying circumstances and in widely different species. There is now good evidence that in dogs, and even in rats, the procedures of classical conditioning may on occasion work by inducing quite elaborate cognitive processes in these animals, such as 'declarative representations' that one event follows another (Dickinson, 1980); or 'expectancies' and 'rich representations' of the food when the buzzer sounds (Mackintosh, 1974; Rescorla, 1979). This does not mean we have to say the same things about sea slugs, even if by some criteria they satisfy our descriptive formulae for classical conditioning.

As with habituation, there may be a set of descriptive rules for classical conditioning, which is extremely useful for theoretical economy and in some cases may help us to make predictions. But for the same descriptive rules there may be a large number of explanations, some of which we have good reason to apply only to a narrow band of experiments. Thus classical conditioning can sometimes be explained as literally a knee-jerk – a muscular reaction which is very directly elicited by a stimulus; often we have good reason to believe that a conditioned stimulus arouses an emotional syndrome, or 'conditioned emotional state', which can be measured by changes in skin resistance, heart rate, and so on; some conditioning may be mainly physiological, in that digestive or metabolic responses are the main things that change; and in yet other cases we have evidence for perceptual or mental associations.

First of all I will describe in more detail some of Pavlov's own results, and then I will list some other experiments in which the effect of stimulus pairings takes these other, much more various, forms.

In the typical Pavlovian experiment a dog is loosely restrained in a stand, with a tube running from its cheek which allows very precise measurement of the amount of saliva it secretes. The dog is hungry, and every five minutes or so a panel just in front of it opens and a small amount of food is pushed out for it to eat. The initial acquisition of a 'conditioned reflex' of salivating to a buzzer is described on p. 6.

Extinction and spontaneous recovery

Suppose that after acquisition, the conditioned stimulus (CS) (the buzzer) is presented over and over again without any food. Should the dog go on salivating? In some circumstances (see chapter 5) conditioned responses may persist for a remarkably long time. However, in experiments using food, the conditioned response usually diminishes quickly when food is withheld and the conditioned stimulus is given by itself. Why is this? If we have assumed that an association between the buzzer and the food has been formed in acquisition, it would seem to be simplest to assume that this association is gradually broken down in extinction – the period when the conditioned response slowly disappears. But the common phenomenon of 'spontaneous recovery' of the conditioned response proves that the original association must somehow have remained intact, despite the waning of response in extinction. Pavlov's explanation was that the original association is not lost, but its effects are counteracted in extinction by a special process of 'inhibition'. The important idea here is that associations built up in conditioning are sometimes not forgotten, even though the responses which occurred initially become suppressed.

Discrimination and generalization

The inhibition concept is often needed to interpret the effects of stimuli which become signals for 'no food'. If a buzzer is used as the signal for food, the dog will at first salivate for almost any sound at all, although the amount of salivation will be less and less for sounds that are more and more unlike the proper signal. The responses to stimuli on the basis of their similarity to one particular signal that has been conditioned may be called 'stimulus generalization'. However, the example here does not mean that dogs are incapable of telling the difference between buzzers and other similar sounds. On the contrary, dogs can make extremely fine auditory discriminations with the benefit of experience, as is evident from the habit seen in many household pets of anticipating the arrival of a familiar person by recognizing an exact pattern of footsteps, or certain particular car noises. Obviously in such cases of exact discrimination, stimulus generalization has been drastically reduced.

Pavlov's way of studying discrimination was to present both positive and negative conditioned stimuli to the same animal. The positive stimulus is followed by food, but the negative stimulus is not. In dogs, this leads very rapidly to them salivating to the positive stimulus, but not to the negative stimulus. If the positive stimulus is, say, a pure tone of middle C, and the negative stimulus is a pure note only an eighth of a tone lower (Pavlov, 1927, p. 136), it is implausible to suppose that they can do this without paying close attention to both stimuli, and the Pavlovian interpretation is that the lower tone has become an inhibitory stimulus.

Inhibitory effects can be transferred from one combination of stimuli to another. Pavlov's example is a dog first trained with three separate positive stimuli: a flashing light, a tone of C sharp and a rotating disc. All these were signals for food and made the dog salivate. Then an 'inhibitory combination' was formed by sounding a metronome along with the sight of the rotating disc, this combination never being followed by food. The dog learned not to salivate to this combination. Then the inhibitory effects of the metronome could be tested by sounding it for the first time along with the other positive signals of the tone and the flashing light. When this was done the usual salivation produced by these stimuli was virtually eliminated. Having taken the precaution of showing that the metronome did not stop salivation before it had been established as an indication of 'no food', Pavlov felt justified in concluding that the metronome had become a 'conditioned inhibitor' (1927, p. 76).

Pavlov's results and the theory of classical conditioning

Pavlov's results with dogs are not in dispute, and his methods and theories have been enormously influential in psychology ever since they were first published (Gray, 1979). However, modern theories of classical conditioning differ markedly from Pavlov's. One difference is that the theories are not now put forward in terms of the physiology of the cerebral cortex, but in more general psychological terms. The second difference is that modern theories are less likely to emphasize the reflex part of conditioned reflexes, and more likely to say that classical conditioning 'enables the animal to learn the relationships between stimulus events in its world' (Gray, 1979, p. 64; Rescorla, 1978, p. 47). Pavlov would probably not have approved of such mentalistic phrases. There are two points to bear in mind.

First, although evidence from experiments like Pavlov's on dogs and other mammals suggests very strongly that these animals learn a good deal more about what is going on than would be required just to salivate or not to salivate to particular stimuli, there are many other experiments, on invertebrates and on mammals with damaged brains, which suggest that the basic phenomena in classical conditioning, such as acquisition, extinction and discrimination, can and do occur in a much more mechanical way. Secondly, Pavlov's own theory, though referring constantly to the conditioning of reflexes, also acknowledged that some very complicated things can happen in conditioning experiments. Pavlov's way of describing the more complicated things was to talk about 'analysis' and 'synthesis' in the nervous system. He was well aware that his dogs did not just discriminate pure tones but could also recognize their own name before and after an experiment, and could be trained during an experiment to distinguish between the same note played on different wind instruments, or between an ascending sequence of notes, *do re me fa*, and the same four notes played in any other order. This is what the 'crowning achievement' of the cerebral cortex is needed for, since dogs which have had operations to remove their auditory cortex can no longer recognize their own names or learn to discriminate between sequences of tones, even though they are 'quite normal' when tested with simple stimuli, such as pure tones of differing pitch (Pavlov, 1927, p. 337; 1955, p. 299).

Thus, one of the reasons why classical conditioning attracts attention in learning theory is that it seems to be widespread, if not universal, occurring in all sorts of species and with all sorts of stimulus and response systems. But we should not forget that although we can often describe the basic acquisition, extinction and discrimination of conditioned responses in the same way, the factor of the complexity of the stimuli and responses involved is enormously variable. Conditioning involves analysis and synthesis, as well as the formation of associations.

Knee-jerk experiments

The human knee-jerk itself is not very reliable in conditioning experiments. But there are some simple motor responses which can be conditioned to occur with simple stimuli in a way which suggests the crudest possible interpretation of conditioned reflexes. Eye-blink conditioning is an example. Many experiments have been performed in which human subjects, made to blink by air puffed into their eyes, show conditioned blinking to a light or tone which precedes the puff. There is little doubt that this is usually an involuntary reflex, although naturally attitudes and instructional sets can make a difference. These factors can be firmly eliminated when conditioning of the third eyelid (nictitating membrane) is obtained in decorticated rabbits. In this case the unconditioned stimulus may be an electric shock to the eye region, but accurate, if slightly slow, conditioning to either a tone or a light has been reported, depending on which is used as the positive conditioned stimulus (Oakley, 1979). Finger-from-flame withdrawal in humans is probably a spinal reflex, and the withdrawal of limbs in response to pain at the extremities may show some marginal conditioning effects in spinal mammals. It has been claimed that conditioning of a spinal reflex has been put to practical use in establishing self-control of the bladder-emptying response in a human paraplegic (Ince *et al.*, 1978). In one patient whose spinal cord had been completely cut half-way down in an accident, it was first established that a mild electric shock to the thigh had no effect on urination. Then it was shown that a stronger shock to the abdomen reliably emptied the bladder (in neither case, of course, could the patient feel anything). This experience itself did not sensitize the bladder-emptying response to the mild thigh shock. But when the thigh shock was applied for a few seconds before and overlapping with the abdominal current (this was done fifty-four times altogether), there appeared to be a conditioning effect, since the bladder now emptied if just the thigh shock was used. The idea behind this was that the patient should be able to empty his bladder at will by pressing a button to deliver his own small thigh shock. There was good evidence for some sort of simple conditioning, even though the factor of the patient raising himself in his chair on his arms during bladder emptying probably helped in the early stages. When there is conditioning without full use of the brain, it is clearly of a fairly low-level type and is not a matter of the bladder (or the nictitating membrane) 'learning the relationship' between the two stimuli.

Metabolic responses

It was observed in Pavlov's laboratories that dogs injected with emetic drugs developed a tendency to vomit at the sight of the syringe, or in response to tones sounded as the original symptoms occurred. In extreme cases dogs vomited simply at the sight of the experimenter who normally gave the injection. This sort of effect may be very general with less noticeable digestive and metabolic responses – it was of course Pavlov's demonstrations that internal bodily responses are under the control of the central nervous system that gained him the Nobel prize. One much studied example is the lowering of blood-glucose level by injections of insulin. Rats given a series of injections of insulin under constant and easily recognizable conditions (with the ringing of a bell or the presence of a strong smell of menthol) will show the full drop in blood-glucose level if they are then injected just with saline solution but under the same conditions. This happens even if, during the conditioning trials but not the test trial, they are injected with glucose as well as insulin, so that the 'unconditioned response' of a peripheral change in blood sugar, does not occur (Woods, 1976).

A more complicated conditioning effect seems to occur in the development of tolerance to drugs such as morphine. In this case it is the tolerance, or anti-drug metabolic response, which seems to become conditioned, so that the tolerance which rats develop when they are always injected in the same room disappears when they are injected with standard doses of morphine in a new room (Siegel, 1976; Kesner and Cook, 1983).

Emotional responses

Specific physiological responses are usually involved in emotional conditioning, and the role of Pavlovian associations in producing fear and anxiety to stimuli which are merely the signals for unpleasant events is the most important aspect of classical conditioning for behavioural theories of the causes and cures of neurosis (see chapters 5 and 9). There is a certain amount of experimental evidence to support the suggestion that human emotions can under some circumstances be conditioned by stimulus pairings. Ohman *et al.* (1975) gave ten electric shocks to the right hands of volunteer subjects, the shock coming in each case just after they had been looking at a coloured slide for eight seconds. This presumably caused some general arousal and apprehension, but the precise response measured was the skin resistance of the left hand. This clearly showed there was an association between the pictures and the shocks, since skin responses started to occur when the pictures were presented. The point of the experiment was that half the subjects saw 'phobic' pictures (of snakes), and the other half saw 'neutral' pictures (of houses or faces). The test came when, after the first ten pictures, no more shocks were given, but the pictures were as before flashed up for eight seconds at a time. The 'neutral' pictures soon stopped eliciting any response, but the 'phobic' pictures carried on causing skin-conductance changes, even after the shock series had been discontinued. This was true for skin responses at the end of the eight-second 'phobic' presentations, and even for a sub-group of subjects who had the electrodes removed from their right hand and were explicitly told that they would not be getting any more shocks. The general argument is that some kinds of stimulus (in this case snakes) are more likely than others to become conditioned to unpleasant forms of autonomic arousal and that, when they do, the association is not necessarily in a rational form.

Although more theoretical attention is given to the conditioning of unpleasant kinds of excitement, more attractive anticipations are not necessarily immune from the effects of involuntary associations. The sight of Botham coming in to bat may be appealing because you have made a close study of cricketing statistics; on the other hand, if you have personally seen one or two mammoth sixes, you may anticipate another one whether or not the recent averages suggest that Botham will be bowled first ball. Few would deny that sexual excitement can be just as irrational as the passions aroused by cricket, and there is experimental evidence that sexual responses can become conditioned to relatively arbitrary stimuli. In one experiment young men in Australia watched a travelogue film of London, which was interrupted every so often by a red circle, which was followed after ten seconds by a clip from a film showing an attractive and nude female figure. Specialized measuring devices showed that changes in the state of the penis, which were initially elicited by the female figure, soon (after five or six trials) started to occur whenever the red circle appeared (Barr and McConaghy, 1972). Two other experiments (Rachman, 1966; Rachman and Hodgson, 1968) were performed before the concept of 'prepared' conditioned stimuli became popular, and used the less arbitrary stimulus of a slide of black knee-length boots before presentations of a selection of arousing nudes. In these cases conditioning proceeded more slowly, and between twenty and sixty trials were needed before male volunteers reached a strict criterion of sexual arousal at the sight of the boots. Extinction of arousal when the boots were no longer followed by other pictures took about the same time, but several subjects reported fantasies involving boots and some showed signs of sexual arousal in response to other forms of footwear, in one case even to sandals. A simple conditioning theory would say that all instances of sexual interest in items of clothing are due to a history of prior associations, but it would be consistent with Pavlov's original speculations if footwear was a special case, since by some evolutionary quirk the representations of the feet in the cerebral cortex are immediately adjacent to those of the genitals.

Perceptual factors

Most forms of perception depend on past experience in some way or another, but conjunctions of two sets of stimuli may have some specific and quite strong effects. If the moving staircases in my London underground station work reliably for a sufficiently long period, then the experience of walking down one which is out of order, and not moving, is extremely strange. Things seem to move which shouldn't, and the normal leg movements used in walking downstairs seem shaky. Feeling movement in an overground station when seated in a stationary train beside another train as it moves out has the same sort of effect. Clearly automatic associations between stimuli in the external modalities of sight and sound and the internal senses of movement and balance are built up during normal experience, and reveal themselves under unusual circumstances. This should count as learning, although it may seem remote from the Pavlovian experiment. A closer analogy is that if a tone is presented to human subjects just before they experience a strong visual after-image (produced by a very bright form followed by darkness), they eventually report that they can see visual images when the tone is turned on without any external stimulus (Davis, 1976). A more peculiar after-image effect arises from staring for a few minutes at a grid of red vertical lines alongside another grid of blue horizontal lines, and then looking instead at similar grids in black and white, when the black and white verticals will look blue and the black and white horizontals will look red (McCullough, 1965). This seems like a fairly ordinary adaptation effect, but it may last for a day, a week or even three months if the pattern of black and white grids are not looked at during that period (Holding and Jones, 1976).

The locus of these perceptual associations is presumably early on in the appropriate sensory pathways. Levey and Martin (1975) report something different, which they call 'classical conditioning of human evaluative responses'. Subjects were given fifty postcards of paintings and scenic photographs, and each selected the two they liked most and the two they liked least. This left a large number about which they felt neutral (on a scale from −100 to +100). They were each shown ten neutral cards followed immediately by their favourites, and then ten neutrals followed by one of the two cards which they most disliked. After this they had to rate the neutral cards again, and it was found that the neutral cards that had been paired with liked cards had gone up 16 points, while the neutral cards that had been paired with strongly disliked scenes or paintings had gone down 31 points. This seems a fairly strong effect, but is it classical conditioning? Well, that depends entirely on your definition of classical conditioning. What Levey and Martin say, reasonably enough, is that if there was any conditioning going on, it was conditioning of 'affective evaluation', or liking, rather than the conditioning of a motor response.

Backward and second-order conditioning

In the typical Pavlovian experiment, the conditioned stimulus has to come before the stronger, unconditioned stimulus, if there is to be any associative effect. One of the things which Levey and Martin (1975) found with their picture postcards was that the disliked stimuli, which seemed to make most difference to the ratings of neutral stimuli paired with them, did this just as much if the disliked cards came first in the pairings and the neutral cards second. It appears that human subjects, at least, can form associations between a succession of stimuli either forwards or backwards. If an advertising company spends large sums of money to put on our television screens a sequence of a girl frolicking on a tropical beach, followed after some seconds by a picture of a packet of cigars, this is not because they hope that you will have an image of the cigars the next time you are frolicking on a tropical beach. It is because they want you to have some image or emotional connotation of the beach and the girl when you are contemplating their cigars, or see a packet on the shelf at the tobacconist's. This applies equally well to scenes of heart-warming rural nostalgia which routinely precede the eating of brown bread – they do not want you to eat more sandwiches when you go to Dorset, but to feel unconsciously heart-warmed when standing in front of their product at the supermarket tomorrow. Even J.B. Watson thought there was more to advertising than this (see chapter 7), and attention-getting and attention-holding may be as important as conditioned associations; but backward conditioning is reasonably well established in human experiments.

A smaller number of experiments demonstrate backward conditioning in non-human mammals. Gray (1975) quotes a Pavlovian experiment, in which dogs were given two stimuli, in either order. One stimulus was a puff of air in the dog's eye, which provoked the response of blinking, and the other was the lifting of the dog's leg by the experimenter, which meant the dog would lift its own leg as soon as it was touched. Whichever order the stimuli were given in, the dogs lifted their legs and blinked when they received either an air puff or a touch on the leg. In another unconventional experiment, Keith-Lukas and Guttman (1975) gave rats just one electric shock to the feet, and soon afterwards a toy rubber hedgehog slowly flew (on wires) across the top of their box. Various control groups made it clear that it was a result of this experience that these rats thereafter steered well clear of the toy hedgehog when it was left stationary in their test cage, with no further shocks given. There is thus no doubt that backward conditioning occasionally occurs, that is emotional- and response-eliciting characteristics of one stimulus are transferred to a second stimulus which follows it instead of preceding it as in the conventional experiment. But it is relatively rare in animal experiments, where the signalling characteristics of conditioned stimuli and the apparently anticipatory functions of conditioned responses are usually obvious. The reasons for this are in most cases to do with the relative strengths of the two stimuli, and the amount of attention given to them (Eysenck, 1975). Once a dog is already eating food, it pays less attention to the subsequent onset of a buzzer. If, as in the usual experiment, it is waiting for food, and notices the buzzer just before the food comes, it is clearly more likely to retain an interest in the buzzer. Much more mechanical processes may favour the forward connections in a somewhat similar way.

Apart from backward conditioning, there are several other procedures which demonstrate the formation of associations between stimuli by more roundabout processes than the basic Pavlovian signalling design, but which are less reliable and produce ostensibly less dramatic experimental results. These 'higher-order' conditioning experiments are dramatic in their own way, however, because they show associative effects on stimuli which have never actually been paired with the primary event. Rescorla (1980) summarized more than a decade of extremely careful and sophisticated experimental work which convincingly demonstrated that not only 'second-order conditioning' but also a number of other subtle associative processes occur in the humble laboratory rat and pigeon. The most straightforward result is as follows. Rats are repeatedly given a ten-second flashing-light signal before food pellets are dropped into their special experimental boxes. A conditioning effect can be measured simply in terms of their general activity (although what they actually do is rear up to look around and then scrabble about in the place where the food pellets are delivered). Now, without getting any more food pellets, they are put in the experimental boxes with the only interest that every now and then a clicker sounds for ten seconds followed by ten seconds of the flashing light. The main result is that the rats come to be very active when the clicker comes on (looking for food pellets then), even though they have never in the experiment had food pellets with the clicker. In fact they become even more active with the clicker than with the light because the clicker seems to be in some sense a more arousing stimulus. If they are then given extra sessions with the light but no food, so that activity in response to the light is extinguished, this has no immediate effect on activity when the clicker is used. Of course they do eventually give up responding to the clicker, and to the clicker followed by the light, if the experiment goes on long enough with no motivating stimuli (food pellets) being delivered (Holland and Rescorla, 1975).

Pavlovian conditioning: summary

The range of results discussed here by no means exhausts all the experiments, or all the theories, that could be put under the heading of classical conditioning. After habituation, when just one stimulus is presented repeatedly, classical conditioning could be said to be the next simplest learning experiment, since only two stimuli are used, one presented just after the other, and the main result is merely that a response which to begin with was given only for the second stimulus moves back to the first stimulus. In terms of mechanisms, this can also be relatively simple, since the basic result can be obtained in sea slugs and perhaps in spinal cords, and certainly in decorticated rabbits. However, although associations between two stimuli, in terms of transferred reflexes, may be fundamental and universal and not very elaborate, the things which become associated are not always so simple. Pavlov called it conditioning when a dog became ill at the sight of a particular person, who had been giving it injections, but the visual recognition of individuals and the internal balances in digestion and metabolism are each in their own way very complicated processes. Apart from the principle of association between two stimuli, a second feature of classical conditioning that covers the whole range of experiments is that whatever it is that is conditioned is involuntary. However, this is a difficult and controversial claim, which belongs partly to the next chapter.

4

Goals, rewards and reinforcements

Learning theorists have always had difficulty in agreeing among themselves whether there is just one principle of learning – perhaps the principle of association, exemplified in classical conditioning – or whether there might be at least two principles, the other usually being the law of effect, as propounded by Thorndike. That there might be an infinite number of principles, varying according to species, experimental apparatus and season of the year, is a nightmare that is occasionally encountered, and put aside with a shudder. Some success is still being achieved by those who stick by a single principle of association, as they are willing to apply the same principle to many different kinds of event. Thus it is possible to claim that Pavlov's dogs learned an association between the buzzer and getting food, while Thorndike's cats, by the same principle of contiguity, learned an association between the response of pawing a latch and the welcome experience of getting out of their box (Mackintosh, 1974, p. 139; Dickinson, 1980). Others believe that there are fundamental differences between Pavlov's dogs and Thorndike's cats; for instance that salivation is involuntary but pawing voluntary (Skinner, 1938), and yet others suggest that each species is a law unto itself (Seligman, 1970; Hinde and Stevenson-Hinde, 1973).

The theoretical ramifications here are difficult, complex and obscure, but in purely practical terms it is possible to make a number of simple distinctions. First of all there is a difference between involuntarily elicited emotional states, or immediate physical reactions, and goal-oriented actions. There is a difference between having an emotion, motive or drive and doing something about it. It is relatively difficult to decide to salivate, or to be angry, or to be anxious, and even more difficult to decide not to salivate or to be angry or anxious, once these reactions have begun. We are usually freer to do what we will than we are to decide what it is that we will. This distinction does not always hold up, especially in animal experiments, but there is a more physiological analogy – the difference between autonomic reactions such as salivation and skin resistance, and skeletal motor reactions such as walking about and making object-directed movements of the front paws. Descriptively, there is a world of difference between making the same old reflexive responses, such as salivation or leg flexion, to new stimuli, and learning new response skills, such as carrying a marble about the cage if you are a rat, balancing a ball on your nose if you are a performing seal, and tying your own shoes if you are a backward child.

Thus there is a case for treating separately the development of new response skills under the influence of reward and punishment, or in the course of striving to achieve more intangible goals, and the shifting about of more reflexive responses and emotional reactions due to Pavlovian associations between stimuli. In learning theory the former are referred to as instrumental learning, or operant conditioning, as opposed to classical conditioning. There is also a case for treating separately many other kinds of learning from experience, such as perceptual learning, the formation of cognitive maps of the environment and the acquisition of knowledge by imitation and by all the resources of human culture – but this takes us even further afield, and I will return to these questions in later chapters.

Stamping-in responses versus forming expectancies

Having assumed that Thorndike's cats were learning in a different way from Pavlov's dogs, can we now say exactly what it was that the cats were learning? Thorndike's law of effect says that the effects or results of the cats' responses, in pulling strings or pressing latches which opened the door to their problem box, gradually stamped in a connection between the stimuli of being in the box and the movements required to pull the strings and press the latches. Descriptively, this is a law of response consequences, which tells us that the probability of an action is determined by its previous outcomes. And this is a pretty good rule of thumb, especially if 'consequences' are interpreted imaginatively. In Skinner's hands, rain dances are performed because of accidental outcomes of rain, work is done because of consequent payments or social credit, and left undone because of the counter-attractions of more rewarding alternatives. But the explanation, in terms of responses being stamped in so that they are automatically elicited by stimuli, has only limited support. Thorndike claimed that the stamping-in was obvious because the cats only learned gradually to make the correct response. This is a false claim for two reasons. First, gradualness does not necessarily imply stamping-in – it could mean, for instance, that there was a gradual change in the cats' ideas – and, second, the cats did not learn gradually anyway (most of them learned very quickly). Thorndike made great play with one animal that learned relatively slowly, in a fairly easy problem box, which could be solved by pulling a loop of string in front of the door. The complete set of latencies of getting out of the box for this animal, in seconds, was 160, 30, 90, 60, 15, 28, 20, 30, 22, 11, 15, 20, 12, 10, 14, 8, 8, 6, 6, 7. This certainly shows some gradual improvements, but note the big difference between the first and second trials. And the average for all the twelve cats tested in this problem box shows a fairly dramatic change between the first two trials and the third (see figure 3).

As Thorndike himself said, it often happened that if a cat was paying attention to what it was doing when the release device worked, 'a single experience stamps the association in so completely that ever after the act is done at once' (Thorndike, 1898, p. 27). If there was an association formed, it was formed very quickly, and modern evidence would suggest that the important thing

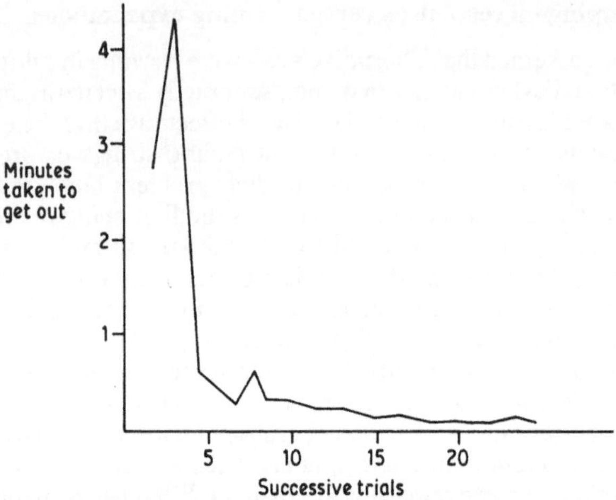

Figure 3 Rapid learning in Thorndike's experiments.
The average time taken by twelve cats to get out of Thorndike's problem box A. Individual cats showed even more striking improvements in speed of making the releasing response from one trial to the next, but some animals made their biggest improvement after the first trial, some after the second and some after the third. (After Thorndike, 1898)

learned by the cats was the association between the escape response and their escape. So when they performed the same response again soon afterwards it was because they expected to get out (Mackintosh, 1974; Dickinson, 1980).

Thus, for cats, we should not assume that rewards work only by stamping in responses; they also work by establishing certain expectancies of reward in the animals, linked with the response it is necessary to perform to get the reward. But, and this is a big but, response consequences do not *always* work by building up an animal's (or a person's) expectancies. There are no experiments yet which show sea slugs pulling strings to get out of marine problem boxes, but there are experiments in which octopuses pull levers to get bits of fish. Operant conditioning is sometimes claimed for a wide variety of invertebrates and, with sufficient dedication on the part of experimenters, decorticated rabbits can be laboriously trained to press levers in Skinner boxes (Oakley, 1979).

Human subjects may by the use of various subterfuges be seen to change the frequency of simple verbalizations like 'Mmm', 'Yes' and 'Go ahead' because these responses have changed social consequences (Rosenfeld and Baer, 1969), while professing no knowledge of either change. One could always appeal to unconscious expectancies and strategies in the learning of human skills and habits, but this still leaves decorticated rabbits, to say nothing of decapitated cockroaches (Horridge, 1962). Oakley (1979) suggests that some forms of response-learning are sub-cortical, which is certainly true, but Dickinson (1980) has put forward a more comprehensive scheme to differentiate between various results of reward training which may be observed in laboratory animals (see also Adams and Dickinson, 1981a). This is based on the distinction between actions and habits, or between 'declarative representations', such as 'pulling the string opens the door', and 'procedural representations', such as 'when in the box, pull the string'. Many lengthy experiments with rats have suggested that trained rats operate according to rules which correspond closely to Thorndike's and others' concepts of stamped-in stimulus-response habits. However, under the right conditions, there are indications that laboratory rats are capable of working according to rules such as 'if you want a sugar pellet, press the lever'. The technique is to train the animals fairly quickly to press a lever to obtain sugar pellets, and then afterwards to give the animals a pile of sugar pellets in a separate cage, with an injection of lithium chloride, which makes them ill. This is well-known as a taste-aversion procedure, which is a reliable way of putting animals off foods which they have formerly liked (Garcia *et al.*, 1977, chapter 5). The rats had learned to press a lever to get sugar pellets, but the assumption now was that they would no longer want sugar pellets. In some cases, especially after long previous training, rats react stupidly and automatically, since they go on pressing the lever even though they would never consume the rewards. In other experiments, however, it is quite clear that the 'devaluation of the reinforcer' by poisoning suppresses the tendency to press the lever (with appropriate controls for any side effects). Thus the conclusion is that the animals were using a declarative rule that 'pressing the lever brings sugar pellets', and when they no longer wanted sugar pellets, they no longer pressed the lever (Adams and Dickinson, 1981b). Responses in rats rewarded by food may either stay goal-oriented, in that changes in the value of the goal very rapidly change the responses, or they may become automatic habits and insensitive to changes in the goals themselves.

The general point is that responses changed by rewards may change for a variety of reasons. It is not enough to know that rewards are effective – we also need to know why they are effective.

Autoshaping and reflexive responses to reward

A very special case of not knowing why rewards work occurred with pigeons rewarded for pecking at keys in Skinner boxes. This set-up was used by Ferster and Skinner (1957) to establish the effects of schedules of reinforcement (see p. 53), on the assumption that presenting a pigeon with food after it had pecked at a key could be the model for all other forms of positive reinforcement, that is attractive rewards given for any response. Although some of the effects of schedules of reinforcement are very general across species, not all are, and it has turned out that the relation between a pigeon's key-pecking and subsequent presentations of grain is very unusual (Terrace, 1981). Pigeons will peck keys in spite of the rewarding properties of food, rather than because of them.

The first finding was that all that is needed to get pigeons to peck the key is to light up the key for a few seconds before each food presentation, following the same sort of rule as is used in classical conditioning (Brown and Jenkins, 1968). Nothing else is needed, for this appears by itself to make the bird spontaneously start pecking at the lighted key, and the effect is called autoshaping. Thereafter, of course, various schedules can be set up in which the pigeon must peck the key in order to get further rewards. But one can also set up the opposite rule, so that if the pigeon does peck at the lighted key food will not be presented on that trial, but if the pigeon is content to wait without pecking the key then food is presented to it for a few seconds at the end of every lighted-key period (which occurs about once a minute on average). This is called an 'omission procedure', since food is omitted when the animal responds. In terms of achieving goals, the best strategy for the birds would be to refrain from pecking at all, but almost all pigeons carry on pecking the key on well over 50 per cent of the trials, thus losing more than half the food which they might obtain by waiting patiently (Williams and Williams, 1969). The usual suggestion is that the pecking is an involuntary and emotional reflexive response, produced by the classical conditioning which results from pairing the key light with the food. This idea is supported by the fact that when, as usually, food is being used, pigeons peck the key with an open beak as if they were trying to eat it, but if water is used instead of food pigeons press the key with a closed beak, as if they were trying to drink from it. It is a fairly safe generalization that in any given experiment on animal learning, evidence can be found for both goal-directed instrumental effects and more reflexive Pavlovian conditioned associations (Mackintosh, 1974, p. 139). Pigeons are certainly not indifferent to the rewarding effects of food and peck far more, according to the various schedules (see pp. 53–5), if pecking produces the goal of food, rather than preventing it.

Also, the lesson to be learned from autoshaping is that pecking for pigeons is exceptional, not that all effects of reward are due to classical conditioning. Since pigeons spend most of their lives pecking things, it is not surprising that this response tends to occur whenever food is in the offing. Other birds, such as crows, do not autoshape in the same way, and indeed most other species, including crows and rats, tend to respond to signals for food by searching for the food, rather than investigating the signal (Lea, 1984). Two experiments in which social behaviour appears demonstrate that the effects of stimulus pairings in reward procedures may be complicated, and certainly reveal large species differences. In Jenkins *et al.*'s procedure (1978) dogs were free to move about in a room in which food was delivered about a metre from a loudspeaker and lamp signal source, which was activated for ten seconds before each food delivery. The dogs differed in their responses, but after some early sniffing at the audio-visual signal a typical pattern was to approach the signal, point at it and playfully bark at it with much wagging of the tail. If the reader thinks it silly of the dogs to have directed such natural social behaviour at an arbitrary signal, consider the swearing, physical abuse or verbal coaxing which people direct at similarly inanimate mechanical objects.

In Timberlake and Grant's experiment (1975), the stimulus presented to rats as a signal that food was about to be delivered was another rat, dropped into the cage. By strict analogy with the pigeon-eating-the-key theory of autoshaping, this should have led to cannibalism, but the result of the 'other rat signals food' association was to increase the amount of friendly social reaction to the new animal, in the accepted rat form of sniffing, pawing and social grooming. The overall message is thus one of species differences, and the integration of reward procedures with the natural behaviour of any particular species. Innate patterns of behaviour have a tendency to assert themselves, and the most successful training methods make use of a species' natural abilities.

Schedules of reinforcement

Given that there are enormous species differences in learning ability, and given that for any species we may need to select its most natural response, there are certain regularities in the relation between the response and experimental schedules of rewards, or reinforcers, which apply across most higher vertebrate species tested (mammals and birds), give or take a certain amount of quantitative variation. The most profound and reliable regularity is also to some extent counter-intuitive and is therefore all the more worthy of note. This is that more is worse, if one is using rewards to generate the maximum amount of behaviour. That needs some qualification: it is more often that is worse, rather than big rewards being worse than small ones, and more often is worse at the end of training than at the beginning. When a learned response is consistently rewarded, absolutely every time it occurs, then if rewards are suddenly stopped it will be almost as if they had never been given; but when rewards are doled out inconsistently and unreliably, then the behaviour so meagrely rewarded is likely to persist through many further trials and tribulations.

There may be natural forces at work in this, since most species have to be accustomed to undertake periods of foraging, chasing or waiting sustained by only the occasional achievement of natural goals, but the study of the 'partial reinforcement effect' in the laboratory allows for discussion of some of the results in terms of experimental variables. The strengthening effects of intermittent reinforcement are apparent in many circumstances, and are said to be readily visible in human gambling. They have been studied extensively in rats running down alleys or through mazes to find food at the goal only if they are in luck on a random experimental sequence. However, they are perhaps most obvious of all in the typical Skinner box experiment. In this the animal in the box makes a single response repeatedly and rewards are occasionally made available by means of a mechanical dispenser of some sort. It is thus possible to institute several simple limiting conditions relating the response to the reward, and many less obvious ones (Ferster and Skinner, 1957). A convenient visual display of the rate at which responses are repeated is obtained by plotting responses cumulatively, as steps up a vertical axis, against the time when they are made, along the horizontal axis. Skinner termed this a 'cumulative record' and it allows quick inspection, although more accurate quantitative methods are used nowadays for experimental work. Typical schedule performance with subsequent patterns of responses in extinction, for five basic schedules of reinforcement, are shown in figure 4, and these schedules are described below.

1 *Continuous reinforcement (CRF):* it is a straight line of shallow angle, with every response rewarded, which quickly flattens out completely when rewards are discontinued in extinction.

2 *Fixed-interval schedules:* training on interval schedules is relatively easy for both trainer and trainee, since only one response is necessary for reward. The interval specified is a minimum, since the rule is that a certain period must elapse after a reward before the next one is obtained, but the next reward is not given until the animal makes its first response after this period is over. On fixed intervals the period is the same every time, say one minute, and the expected result (for a rat or a pigeon after several hours of experience) is that an animal somehow uses a biological clock in order to vary its response rate, responding faster and faster as time passes since the last reinforcement and the next reward becomes due. Even in the absence of rewards, in extinction, this patterning of behaviour is sustained, and gradual accelerations of response rate can be observed. It has been shown that the passage of time, rather than the chaining together of responses, is the important variable, and the relation of response output to internal timing processes continues to be a topic for investigation (Roberts and Church, 1978).

3 *Variable-interval schedules:* if the specified minimum interval between any two rewards is varied at random, the time at which a

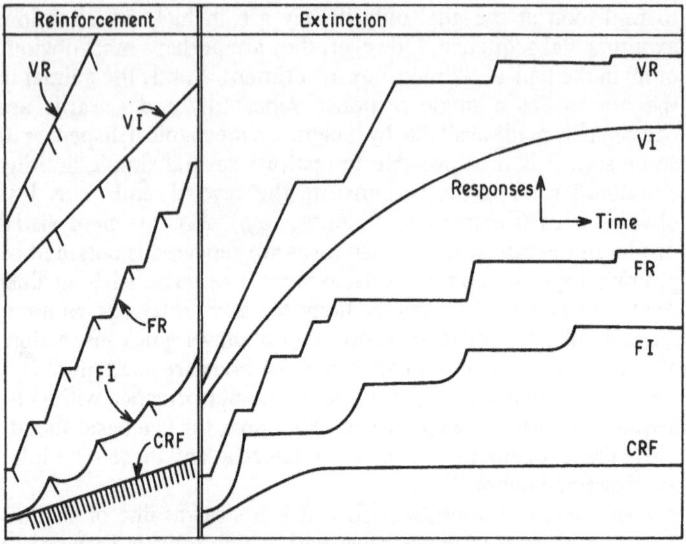

Figure 4 Cumulative records of reinforced responding and extinction with basic schedules of reinforcement.

reward can be obtained must be unpredictable, and a steady and fast rate of response is eventually obtained, indicating either that the animal expects reward at any time or that consistent and sustained patterns of responding have become habitual. There is still a slight tendency for response rate to increase as time passes since the last reinforcement. When all reinforcements are discontinued, response rate declines very slowly and gradually.

4 *Fixed-ratio schedules:* care is necessary for training on fixed-ratio schedules. The rule is that the animal must make a certain fixed number of responses for each reward. An animal first reinforced for every response, and then put immediately on the task of making a hundred responses per reward (FR100) would almost certainly give up. However, suppose that the task requirement is increased gradually, or that, as in Skinner's original experiment (1938), the animals are first trained on an interval schedule (which allows for backsliding because rewards are always available at some point for just one response). In this case ratios of tens or hundreds may be undertaken by rats and pigeons, and a ratio of

120,000 responses per (large) reward has been reported for a chimpanzee (Findley and Brady, 1965). The organization of responses is very obvious when an animal has learned a fixed-ratio schedule, since it pauses completely after each reinforcement, and then reels off the required fixed number of responses very rapidly. It is clear from the persistence of such step-wise patterns in extinction, and from more detailed experiments, that the grouping of responses approximates the number required, and in some cases there are indications that an animal comes to expect reward when this fixed number has been completed (Adams and Walker, 1972).

5 *Variable-ratio schedules:* these are the closest to gambling schedules, since responses must be made in order to obtain reward, but each response has a low probability of a successful outcome. The faster the animal responds, the more often it will be rewarded, and thus very high response rates may be obtained. However, if, at random, rewards become very scarce indeed, animals may show signs of 'ratio strain' and respond only in bursts (Ferster and Skinner, 1957).

Biofeedback and response skills

It is often possible in everyday life to distinguish between the motives for attempting a task and the factors which allow for mastery of it. In many competitive sports, the rewards for engaging in them may have to do with the excitement of competition, the joys of winning, love of the game itself or its social fringe benefits, whereas the development of the skills necessary for taking part may involve many hours of tedious and lonely practice. Rewards obtained by exercising a skill, although useful in inducing further efforts, may not make any difference to proficiency: no amount of celebration surrounding the achievement by a golfer of a hole in one is likely to improve his swing, although it may encourage him to spend more time playing. On the other hand the swing may be improved by certain prompts and advice, such as suggestions about changes of grip, keeping the head down and so on, which are not much fun in themselves.

However, a law of response consequences may often be applied to skills. Feedback, both internal and external, which supplies information about what is actually being done is usually necessary to provide structure and organization in response output. Moreover, knowledge of results in some form or other is logically essential in the later stages – it would be impossible for a golfer to get very far if he never ever knew what happened to the balls he hit. Even in the golfer, it is possible to distinguish between two aspects of response consequences, the motivational and the informational, however much these are intertwined in practice. Information that you are doing something the wrong way may be just as useful as the information that you are getting it right – in both cases being right or wrong can have motivational effects. However, small-scale detailed information such as that gained internally by proprioception, or that which improves split-second timing when you succeed in keeping your eye on the ball, have beneficial effects on performance, and these are out of all proportion to their influence on motivation, which may be negligible.

A special case of response consequences occurs in the therapeutic technique called 'biofeedback'. Nature has not seen fit to provide us with a great deal of detailed feedback about the state of our internal organs or the volume of our glandular secretions. We are, thankfully, not usually aware of how much we are salivating, how fast our heart is beating, what our blood pressure is, or what is happening to our skin-conductance response. These are all controlled by the autonomic part of the nervous system, and this does not have as much by way of internal and unconscious neural control circuits as does the skeletal system for balance and movement. It is partly because of this lack of internal feedback that it is extremely difficult to learn to voluntarily control autonomic responses such as heart rate. After years of dedication and self-denial yogis in India can do it; and it is easy enough to raise one's heart rate by running up and down the stairs, but this is not the same thing as direct voluntary control of heart rate, in the same way that we have direct voluntary control of whether to run upstairs or not.

A short cut to a measure of increased self-control over bodily states of the yogi type is to provide external feedback by electronic means. Subjects, or patients, can be provided with an egg-like object to hold in their hand, which emits a tone of increasing pitch when skin resistance is lowered by anxiously sweating palms. Lights can be made to flash if blood pressure gets too high, or for experimental purposes a speedometer needle can be put in front of patients which gives an exact read-out of their moment-to-moment heart rate. With these aids, people have a much better chance of learning to keep their skin resistance, blood pressure, or heart rate within prescribed limits, although biofeedback of this kind is by no means a universal panacea for disordered autonomic activity (Yates, 1980). How biofeedback helps is a difficult and complicated question. Both mental and physical strategies are involved, since autonomic responsiveness can vary according to voluntary breathing patterns, posture, and degree of muscle relaxation; and according to calming or exciting trains of thought and spoken or unspoken verbal rituals.

It is almost certainly not true that biofeedback works by directly reinforcing autonomic responses, according to the principles of reward and punishment and instrumental learning. Of course motivation is important, and so is practice. People have to make efforts to 'keep the needle on the right' or 'make the tone stay low', but to do this they can learn cognitive and muscular intervening states. And so can animals. It is still sometimes claimed that direct reward and punishment of autonomic responses was demonstrated by certain experiments reported some time ago by Neal Miller and Leo DiCara on rats whose entire skeletal musculature had been paralysed by the drug d-tubocurarine (e.g. DiCara and Miller, 1968, Miller and DiCara, 1967). All such effects are either fraudulent or artifactual. Undrugged rats respond very well to biofeedback procedures, and previous experience prior to paralysis may reveal itself in the drugged state. But although Miller himself is a scientist of undoubted integrity and repute, the early experiments on curarized rats can all be dismissed. There are many technical difficulties associated with continuous adjustments to the artificial respiration of curarized animals. No one else has been able to repeat the original results despite enormous efforts in other laboratories, DiCara for one reason or another committed suicide, and Miller now says 'it is prudent not to rely on any of the experiments on curarized animals for evidence on the instrumental learning of visceral responses' (1978, p. 376).

Cognitive processes in animal learning

There have been two main developments in the study of animal learning over the past decade. One is the realization that some responses are learned more easily than others. Not only are whole body movements and object manipulations learned more easily under the influence of external rewards and punishments than the complex internal balances of the internal organs, but for each species certain kinds of natural action are more readily associated with biologically appropriate goals and deterrents (Lea, 1984; Walker, 1975). The second trend is that far greater emphasis than formerly has been placed on inner cognitive processes as important determinants of those learned actions (Mackintosh, 1974; Hulse *et al.*, 1978; Dickinson, 1980; Roitblat *et al.*, 1983; Walker, 1983). Much of the evidence which has supported this trend has come from experiments in which reward procedures are subtly modified in ways which reveal the importance of internal descriptions of outer events, expectancies for the immediate future and memories of the immediate past to a greater extent than was apparent in the initial experiments of Thorndike and Skinner. Detailed treatment of this topic can be found elsewhere, but the experimental techniques can be summarized in terms of spatial learning, perception and memory.

Spatial learning – mazes and maps

Tolman's interpretation of his maze experiments – that they indicate that rats form cognitive maps of their environment independently of imposed rewards and punishment – has been broadly supported (O'Keefe and Nadel, 1978). A new technique which produces easily replicated results is the radial maze (Olton, 1979). In this, eight arms are laid out like the spokes of a cartwheel, but with no outer perimeter. A single food pellet is placed at the end of each arm, and in the basic experiment a rat is simply put in the middle of the maze and allowed to go forth and back along each spoke, retrieving the food pellets. The experimental result is the fact that it almost never retraces its steps. Thorndike's stamping-in principle would suggest that the animal would have to repeat each rewarded response or respond at random. Searching by smell is not the answer: crude controls initially included drenching the whole maze in aftershave, which the rats found unpleasant but not confusing. More sophisticated controls (including confining the rat at the central axis while the arms were rotated, or already tried arms switched with untried ones) all indicate that rats make use of visual landmarks to distinguish where they have already been from where food pellets remain to be found. Animals must have both some sort of mental map of their world and also something analogous to a working memory, which records what they have recently been doing in that world.

Perception and pattern recognition

Countless experiments confirm the intuition that higher animals as well as people must have some way of picking out transiently relevant details from the booming and buzzing confusion which would surround them if all sensory channels remained permanently open. This applies within sensory modalities, as well as between them. If tones predict rewards, then pigeons will pay more attention to tones than they would otherwise. But equally, if shapes predict rewards one minute, and colours the next, then both pigeons and monkeys learn to select shapes irrespective of colour, or colour irrespective of shape, as appropriate.

Slightly more surprising is the finding that pigeons can somehow learn to distinguish As from 2s, irrespective of which of dozens of different type faces they might suddenly be presented with (Morgan *et al.*, 1976). Pigeons also learn to distinguish photographs of one person (in any of 100 poses) from photographs of other individuals in the same range of surroundings and activities; holiday slides which contain people from those which do not; slides with trees from slides without trees; silhouettes of oak leaves from silhouettes of leaves from any other species (Herrnstein *et al.*, 1976; Cerella, 1979). All of this goes to show that stimulus learning is separate from response learning, and that recognizing familiar objects and individuals, which is an imperative fact of life for most species, requires the building-up, as a result of learning from experience, of a vast array of elaborate internal descriptions (Walker, 1983). Whenever rewards are given, this will not merely motivate and inform rewarded responses, it will also affect the attention and perception of the rewarded subject.

Memory and expectancies

Clearly, spatial and perceptual learning, as well as the learning of precise and orderly response skills, requires the retention of information in some complicated forms. The way in which retained information controls current actions is a very tricky subject, and in most cases it can be assumed that animal behaviour is impelled by needs of the moment, rather than constructed from the recall of past history and anticipatory speculation. However, Mackintosh (1974) and Adams and Dickinson (1981b) suggest that there are instances where past experience appears to result in the formation of sensible expectancies and guesses by laboratory rats. Also, specialized experimental techniques have revealed that detailed information about previous episodes of experience sometimes determines choices made by laboratory animals (Medin *et al.*, 1976; Roitblat *et al.*, 1983).

Weismann *et al.* (1980) conclude from a careful study in which different orders of coloured lights were presented to pigeons that 'animals have more than a succession of feelings – they have a feeling of succession'. This is one way in which memorial processes can be expected to be utilized by many animal species: the continuity and ordering of perceptions over time, and the ordering and sequencing of behavioural output, are extremely general requirements. However, this would not imply much by way of remembered knowledge of events. Experiments on monkeys and apes suggest that our closest relatives have the closest approximations to our own memories, even if lacking in the ability to put memories in a verbal code. Without such verbal coding there is no doubt even more of a memorial vacuum than the one we would experience if we were prevented from ever consulting our books, notes, photocopies, file cards and minutes.

The visual memory of pig-tailed macaque monkeys for pictures of coffee mugs, shoes, spectacles, screw-drivers and other human artefacts is about 80 per cent reliable over a period of two days (Overman and Doty, 1980). This is not as good as human subjects given the equivalent test, since they were 100 per cent correct, but the pig-tailed macaques neither know names for these objects nor do they wear shoes or spectacles or drink from coffee mugs, and they understandably pay far less attention to the pictures. The monkeys only paid attention at all because they were allowed to drink orange juice from a tube when they touched the correct pictures.

It is no easy matter to interpret the results obtained with tests of animal memory, but the results seem to imply recognition processes which decay with time and which occur in some way or other in all laboratory birds and mammals. Such memory processes may have many natural functions – although squirrels may often forget where they store their nuts, they presumably remember at least some of the time. Birds which store nuts or seeds often seem to make few mistakes in finding them, and the marsh tit has performed well on this task in a rigorous experimental test (Shettleworth and Krebs, 1982). However, memory is clearly most human-like in monkeys and apes. On such tasks as sorting pictures into different object categories, or sorting nuts, bolts and washers into different piles according to size and type, young chimpanzees may perform as well as human 3- or 4-year-olds (Hayes and Nissen, 1971). Baboons (Beritoff, 1971) and chimpanzees (Menzel, 1978) remember where they have seen food being hidden for minutes and hours, and they remember for weeks and months exactly where in a particular room they themselves once found food, never having been back to that room in the intervening period.

The many attempts to train chimpanzees to communicate by gestural sign language, or by manipulating visual symbols for objects and actions, have not demonstrated any ability on their part to acquire the syntax and grammar which is characteristic of human speech. It is, however, possible to interpret the results of these attempts as further support for the proposition that simian intelligence includes a large measure of cognitive understanding by monkeys and apes of their experience of the world about them, and that therefore a theory of how behaviour is affected by experience cannot afford to leave out the effect of rewards on memory of past events and expectations of future ones (Shettleworth and Krebs, 1982; Walker, 1983).

Conclusions

It should go without saying that the application of learning theory to human behaviour will have to be far more circumspect today than it was for Thorndike and Skinner. For the theory of learning by reward, in order to account for experimental evidence obtained from both rats and chimpanzees, has had to develop from Thorndike's concept of stamped-in stimulus-response connections to the consideration of perceptual categorization, the organization of memory, and expectancies which are derived from if-then declarative representations of the relation between responses and reinforcements. But we should be careful not to forget that, in practical terms, experimental results stand apart from theory. There is little in subsequent work to deny the empirical generalization which impressed itself on the earlier learning theorists that, however it may come about, the effect of reward procedures on future behaviour is profound, dramatic and pervasive.

5

Punishment, avoidance, conflict and anxiety

Apart from administrations of morphine, repeated beyond the point of addiction, no motivating event used in animal experiments has as long-term an effect on future behaviour as the delivery of painful electric shocks. Rats allowed to press a lever which causes morphine to be pumped into their bloodstreams become addicted, and even after long abstinence and treatments with methodone, which reduces withdrawal symptoms, never lose the tendency to try out the same lever, even months after their physical dependence. The only other long-term effect that can be compared to this is when (other) rats are given strong shocks for pressing a lever, or dogs learn to jump a barrier to escape from shocks. As a consequence, the rats may never again approach the site of their punishing experience, and the dogs may never cease to jump over the barrier, even though no further shocks are experienced (Church, 1969; Solomon *et al.*, 1953; Solomon, 1964).

There are ethical arguments against exposing experimental animals to this sort of procedure, and also against the use of punishment as an educational or legal sanction. And, as human experience shows even more vividly than animal experimentation, the use of punishing events to control behaviour may have many counter-productive outcomes, such as the build-up of tolerance to punishment, the development of anger and resentment against punishing agencies and other things associated with them, and debilitating physical and emotional disorders in those punished. The desire to reduce all punishing events to a minimum both in the animal laboratory and in human societies is therefore admirable, and we have no wish, I hope, to encourage beatings in school or to return to the Norman and Tudor traditions of hanging our most punishable miscreants in public until they are too feeble to struggle and then burning their detached entrails and genitals in front of them while they are still alive.

But although the desire to downgrade the importance of punishment may be commendable, it is not possible to defend seriously the position taken by Thorndike (1932) and Skinner (1953), that while rewards strengthen behaviours, punishing events have no equivalent deterrent effects on responses which produce them. At least as far as animal experimentation goes, there is more evidence to support a symmetrical view of reward and punishment, such as that of Mackintosh (1974), who says that just as rewarded responses are generally performed because of 'the expectation of an increase in incentive', so 'responses accompanied by an increase in anticipation of aversive reinforcement are thereby suppressed' (pp. 269, 299).

The suppressing effect of punishing stimuli on previously rewarded activities is illustrated by the experiment quoted by Church (1969). In this, several groups of rats were first trained for a short time to press a lever for food rewards, with a fixed-interval schedule of reinforcement (see p. 53). Then they were given nine sessions of testing in which no further rewards were delivered. For the first fifteen minutes of the first session every lever press resulted in a shock, different groups receiving different levels of shock. The effect of this was that responding was suppressed according to the strength of the punishment given.

Approach and avoidance conflict

If responses have previously been rewarded, and are punished mildly, there is no reason why they should be suppressed completely. Any symmetrical theory of reward and punishment will have to predict that response output should reflect the balance between previous rewards and punishments. Broadly speaking, choices tend to be systematically influenced by the intensity of previous attractive and aversive experiences, as these theories suggest, although there are many exceptions. Certainly the deterrent effect of shocks on a rat's approach to a goal is roughly in proportion to the intensity of the shock, and, at a given level, punishment may be overcome by a large enough food reward. Natural defensive responses may blur the issue (see below), but a considerable body of data reported by Miller (1944) was based on the natural tendency of hungry rats to approach a source of food, but avoid a source of danger.

In a typical experiment, rats were allowed to run back and forth along a plank or alley, at one end of which there was a goal box in which they were both fed and shocked. The net attractiveness of the goal box was assessed both by how far they approached it when placed at the other end of the alley, and by how hard they would pull towards it when placed at a certain point while in a harness attached to a calibrated spring. This allowed for independent assessment of approaches to food and avoidances of shock as well as of the combined effects of both. Under these circumstances, with rats, the factor of distance from the goal seems to be more important for aversive than for attractive stimuli. They would pull almost as hard to get towards the food from a long distance away as from close up. However, while exerting their strongest efforts to get further away when placed close to the source of shock, they showed a very sharp decline in these efforts as their distance from the anxiety-provoking stimulus increased. Thus it was said that the avoidance gradient was steeper than the approach gradient. Obviously enough, pulls towards food were proportional to degree of hunger, and pulls away from shock were proportional to the intensity of previously experienced shocks. With an appropriate combination of hunger and shock level, and with both food and shock having been experienced in the same goal, it was possible to confirm conflict between approach and avoidance tendencies; the rats would start running towards the goal, and then slow down and stop, at a distance depending on the balance between hunger and fear. Animals varied a good deal in their exact reactions, but many vacillated in a rather human manner (Miller, 1944, p. 438).

Escape and avoidance training

In the learning of particular responses to escape from and avoid electric shocks, the importance of natural patterns of behaviour (called 'species-specific defence responses': Bolles, 1978) is even more obvious than in other forms of animal learning.

Pigeons will peck at almost anything in surroundings where food has been recently presented, but can be trained to peck keys to escape or avoid shocks only with the utmost difficulty. Avoidance of dangerous places, by flying, running or any available form of locomotion is easy to obtain in most species, but arbitrary responses such as lever-pressing or key-pecking are likely to be hampered by competition from these natural responses or from others such as freezing or keeping very still. Certainly, rats will learn to press levers to turn off shocks, and even to lower the frequency of an intermittent train of shocks, whether at fixed or random intervals (Sidman, 1953; Herrnstein, 1969), but behaviours which involve the avoidance of dangerous places are more revealing. In a Skinner box, rats learn best to press a lever to avoid floor shocks if the lever press leads to the motorized insertion into the box of a shelf onto which they can jump (Baron *et al.*, 1977).

Much of the data on which theories of avoidance learning are based have been obtained using a device known as a 'shuttle box'. This is simply a box divided into two, sometimes with a barrier or door between the two compartments, shocks being deliverable through the floor of either compartment independently. Sometimes shocks are always delivered in the same compartment, and animals thus learn to get out of this whenever they are put in it ('one-way avoidance'). In other cases shocks are delivered to either compartment and are preceded by a sound or light signal, and animals learn to shuttle out of whichever compartment they are in when the signal is given (called 'two-way avoidance'). In all cases of successful avoidance learning, what animals learn is to avoid contact with the motivating stimulus. This is one of many important differences between attractive and aversive stimuli, or reward and punishment, as motivating events for learning. With attractive stimuli, learning leads to increased contact with the motivating event, and consequently to sustained exposure to important information, whereas with aversive stimuli, patterns of avoidance may be construed as lack of reality testing, and it is inevitable that successful learning leads to decreased exposure to information about the reason for learning (Mowrer, 1969). To be on the safe side, it would be best to avoid doing things which *might* be dangerous, and in this way avoidance strategies can become self-sustaining in a way in which reward-seeking strategies cannot.

The only theory of avoidance-learning worth considering here is the 'two-factor theory' which supposes that both Pavlovian conditioning and instrumental learning are involved – these are the two factors (or two processes; Gray, 1975). Pavlovian conditioning means that stimuli associated with shock or other forms of unpleasantness come to elicit a motivational state of fear or anxiety, and the instrumental learning consists of the animal's attempts to lessen the fear and anxiety. This deals reasonably well with successful avoidance-learning, for example when animals run away from dangerous places. Particular test cases attempt to separate out the (classical) learning of fear from the (instrumental) avoidance of fear. Thus Miller (1948) shocked rats in one compartment of a shuttle box, and then locked the rats in that compartment. No further shocks were given, but escape was possible by the turning of a wheel which opened a door, allowing the rats to get out into the other compartment. They quickly learned to do this. It seems plausible to assume that being in the compartment in which they had previously been shocked was in some sense unpleasant, and this provided the motive for learning to turn the wheel to get out of it. Herrnstein (1969) and Mackintosh (1974) suggest that because rats will also learn to press levers to reduce shock frequencies while staying in the same box, the hypothesis of 'conditioned fear' is not strictly necessary. But since they have to talk instead about 'a discriminative stimulus for the avoidance response' (Herrnstein, 1969, p. 49), or 'a decrease in proximity to aversive reinforcers' and 'an increase in anticipation of aversive reinforcement' (Mackintosh, 1974, pp. 314, 299), their scepticism seems singularly misguided.

Taste-aversion learning and other defensive behaviours

Since the two-factor theory includes the idea of associative shifts in natural emotions aroused by unpleasant or feared events, it is not difficult to incorporate within it phenomena which point up the importance of natural, species-specific reactions to aversive stimuli. It is now commonly accepted that associative shifts themselves will be partly determined by the innate propensities of the species involved. Taste-aversion learning is in fact widespread across species, although there are differences in detail. About 70 per cent of people in a psychiatric survey of human food aversions said that their aversion dated from particular experiences of feeling ill after eating food they were now averse to (Garcia *et al.*, 1977). A similar phenomenon, sometimes called the 'Garcia effect', has been observed in many animals (Garcia, 1981).

In the original experiments rats were allowed to lap at bottles of sweet- or salty-tasting water, laps being accompanied by clicks and flashing lights. Then, either electric shocks accompanied lapping, or the animals were made ill by radiation treatment or by lithium chloride added to the water. On subsequent tests shocked rats avoided lapping from bottles if this caused clicks and flashing lights, but drank freely of quiet but tasty water, whereas the animals which had suffered intestinal distress were unconcerned by clicks and flashes, but avoided drinking water which tasted like the water they had drunk before becoming ill. Illness seems to be naturally attributed to tastes, and peripheral pain to audio-visual signals (Garcia and Koelling, 1966). There is also no need for the taste experience to be contiguous in time with illness – animals made ill seem to be put off whatever it was they have last eaten, however long that was ago (Garcia *et al.*, 1966).

The 'Garcia effect' can be a very strong one, apparently counteracting other natural behaviours such as hunting. (Male rats become averse to copulation if this behaviour is repeatedly followed by illness: Peters, 1983.) In an interesting twist, wolves can be quickly deterred from attacking sheep by once being given lithium chloride tablets mixed with chopped mutton and wrapped in sheep's clothing. After being made ill by this concoction, wolves and coyotes who previously attacked and killed live sheep, first made half-hearted attacks and then gradually became more and more submissive, eventually running away or lying down when lambs approached them. Garcia's theory to explain these results is that the aversive experience after eating poisoned mutton wrapped in sheepskin leads to a 'hedonic shift' with respect to sheep generally (Garcia *et al.*, 1977). There are also 'conditioned disgust responses' since coyotes will urinate on, roll on or bury fresh meat, whether rabbit or lamb, to which they have previously been averted. Similarly, rats which have been shocked by touching a particular object in their home cage will urinate on it or pile sawdust or any other movable materials over it (Terlecki *et al.*, 1979). Reactions to aversive events, whether conditioned or unlearned, are not just a matter of arbitrary reactions to emotional distress, but include a variety of related motives and response tendencies whose provenance is innate.

Self-punishment

We can usually appeal to innate factors to help explain the many experiments in which animals appear to expose themselves to painful stimuli unnecessarily, either by failing to learn an avoiding response which is unnatural to them or, more dramatically, by the persistent performance of a natural response which is being punished – self-punishment, or the 'vicious circle phenomenon' (Brown, 1969). In an investigation in which dogs were trained to jump over a barrier in a two-way shuttle box in order to avoid very intense shock, most dogs continued to jump the barrier whenever the signal was given, though shocks would no longer occur if they stayed put. In an attempt to decondition the jumping, a short shock was given always in the side the dogs jumped *to*, not in the side they were jumping away from. Out of 13 dogs, 3 stopped jumping, but the other 10 carried on jumping even more quickly and vigorously. Clearly it would have been difficult, under conditions of high emotional arousal, and with the natural response of jumping, for the animals to distinguish the relation between the location of the shock and their jumping behaviour. There is also the relief, or 'safety-signal', theory, which suggests that when a short shock comes to an end, the fact that it has ended somehow reinforces even the responses which brought about the aversive experience. However, the importance of the persistence of natural reactions, perhaps just because they are natural, is supported by the following finding. The dogs were prevented from jumping the barrier by use of a glass screen, so that they experienced the warning signal but no shock. Thus they were exposed to the reality that not jumping was objectively safe. Nevertheless, this did not prevent them from starting to jump again as soon as the barrier was removed (Solomon *et al.*, 1953).

A fairly similar result was obtained with rats by Melvin and Smith (1967), using a one-way avoidance response. The rats were trained to run down a 4-foot alley. They were put in a starting box, and when a trap door opened they had five seconds to run to a safe goal box at the end before the whole alley was electrified. That was the training experience. Two groups were then compared: in one group no more shocks were given, and these rats moved more and more slowly; in the other, the second foot of the alley was always electrified – these rats would have been better off not running down the alley at all, but they continued to run, even faster than in avoidance training. Moreover, when the conditions were switched, both groups kept running, but the fastest running of all was observed in the rats who had been through the phase of running slowly and not being shocked, and then were given the condition in which just the second foot of the alley was always live. Instead of avoiding shock by staying put, by the time they had had ten trials of this final phase they were running down the alley at a speed of 5 feet a second (very fast for a rat).

Passive responses as well as active ones may appear to be self-punitive. Rats required to press a lever in a Skinner box in order to turn off shock have a natural and understandable tendency to hold the lever pressed firmly in the down position for long periods. If, at the same time as they are required to escape occasional shocks by depressing the lever, they are given additional short sharp shocks every 2 or 3 seconds for as long as the lever is held down, this does not induce the most effective behaviour, which would be brief lever presses. Rather, rats hold the lever down for even longer periods, thus receiving thousands of additional punishments (Migler, 1963).

A more peculiar result, originally obtained by Muenzinger (1934), is that rats who learn to run always towards light in a one-choice T-maze to obtain food actually learn faster if they are given shocks along with the food, or almost anywhere else in the maze, than if they are trained only with rewards. Although there are differing explanations for this effect, all bear some relation to the idea that aversive stimuli may enhance attention or add distinctivenness to the environment (Fowler and Wischner, 1969). All such generalizations depend a great deal on the intensity of the stimuli involved, but for relatively mild motivating stimuli it is worth bearing in mind that one way in which rewarding and punishing stimuli can be said to have identical effects is that they both command attention.

Stress, learned helplessness and depression

Again taking due allowance for emotional intensity, it is incontrovertible that one way in which attractive and aversive stimuli can be said to have opposite effects is that rewards engender health and happiness while punishments endanger these desirable states. There are, however, a number of confounding factors to do with predictability, uncertainty, and the nature of the activities which are rewarded or punished. Although prolonged exposure to pain or other intensely unpleasant states of affairs can generally be expected to produce stress at the physiological level, measurable in animals by stomach ulceration, weight loss and mortality, the most influential hypothesis in this area is that the psychological factor of being unable to react positively to aversive events contributes both to the physiological effects of stress and to the future emotional and motivational characteristics of the individuals concerned. This is Seligman's 'learned helplessness' theory. Animal experiments may be quoted both for and against it, and the application of the theory to the phenomena of human depressive states has received much attention (Seligman *et al.*, 1968; Seligman, 1975; Abramson *et al.*, 1978; Miller and Norman, 1979).

If dogs are strapped in a harness and given inescapable shocks, they perform poorly in subsequent tests of their ability to learn active responses to avoid shock. Similarly rats or gerbils, given tasks of escaping from or avoiding shocks which they are unable to master, will thereafter fail on relatively easy tasks of shock avoidance which other animals without the history of failure are able to learn (Seligman and Beagley, 1975; Brown and Dixon, 1983). The argument is not so much over these data, although the results of the experiments are often difficult to interpret in terms of the relevant experimental variables, but over the details of the explanation. In some cases a factor of temporarily emotional or physical exhaustion may be responsible for the results obtained in animal experiments. The generalizations made to human depression may therefore be questioned, although emotional exhaustion is not of negligible influence for people (Miller and Norman, 1979). Clearly, however, there may be simpler explanations of the animal results than 'giving-up', self-blame, inadequate self-concepts and other cognitive factors which may present themselves in human psychiatric cases.

An intermediate level of explanation, which appears to be appropriate to many of the animal experiments, is that during the phase of inescapable punishment, or of insoluble escape tasks, animals learn to be inactive and passive, by innate crouching or freezing or as a more general response strategy. The main evidence for this is that 'helpless' rats, unable to learn the active avoidance responses of running or lever pressing, were not impaired at the task of avoiding shock by gently pushing a small panel placed just in front of their nose (Glazer and Weiss, 1976). It seems probable that passive response strategies, instead of (or perhaps as well as) more general emotional effects, are responsible for the learned helplessness phenomenon in animals. But it can be pointed out (in favour of Seligman's application of the theory of learned helplessness to human emotions) that inactivity and even extreme slowness of normal movements are sometimes associated with psychiatric depression.

Conclusions

The imposition of aversive stimuli on animals is generally to be frowned on, but results from such experiments have led to developments in learning theory which must be noted. According to the two-factor theory, aversive stimuli give rise to states of fear and anxiety, which may be conditioned to other signals when there is some natural connection involved. Conditioned fear and anxiety may then impel the learning of new responses which give relief from these unpleasant inner states, and also arouse other natural emotions and innate responses. This theory has been particularly important as an influence on behavioural explanations and recommendations concerning the origin and treatments of neurosis, which are discussed in later chapters.

6

Pavlov's applications of his conditioned reflex theory

The last recorded publication in Pavlov's official *Selected Works* (1955) is a letter dated 7 January 1936 (a few weeks before his death) and addressed to a gathering of 'leading miners' in the Donetz basin in the Ukraine. These leading miners were the first Stakhanovites, heroes of Soviet labour who, leading a team of assistants, worked exceptionally hard, and thus gained official prestige and financial rewards (though not always the affection of their assistants – as Wadja's film *Man of Marble* shows). In immediately preceding extracts from his speeches, Pavlov comments on the fact that around that time the Soviet government was pouring millions of roubles into his laboratories and extending his research station at Koltushi, outside Leningrad, so that it became a 'scientific city' (Asratian, 1953). One is obviously led to wonder whether Pavlov's scientific psychology had any influence on contemporary methods of industrial and agricultural management or propaganda techniques in the Soviet Union. According to Gray (1979), the answer is that such influence was probably very marginal and indirect, since Pavlov's psychology was not endorsed by the Soviet Academy of Sciences until 1950.

It is, however, worthy of comment that Pavlov had considerable eminence in his own country, as well as internationally, following the award of his Nobel prize in 1904; and his theoretical terminology and experimental techniques spread to the applied human sciences (e.g. Luria, 1966). Pavlov himself took an interest in several areas of human psychology: types of temperament, or personality; psychiatric disturbance, especially schizophrenia; and hypnosis. He read a paper in Madrid in 1903 on 'Experimental psychology and psychopathology in animals', and from 1918 began attending psychiatric clinics to observe human patients. In the 1920s he took an increasing interest in psychiatric problems. Even though he was then in his seventies, he remained intellectually vigorous and productive, and he was of course still head of a very large research team, with excellent facilities. As part of the New Economic Policy in 1921 Lenin had personally signed a decree stipulating that the most favourable conditions should be established for Pavlov's work (including double food rations for Pavlov and his wife, and maximum equipment for their apartment as well as the laboratory).

In the foreword by Popov and Rokhlin to a selection of articles under the heading of *Psychopathology and Psychiatry*, published in Moscow in 1962, there is the rather sinister remark that the articles are especially important for 'problems of so-called borderline psychiatry' (Pavlov, 1962, p. 9). Since Soviet psychiatry has become notorious in the past two decades for treating political dissidents as schizophrenics, it should be noted that Pavlov's main suggestion to Soviet psychiatrists in 1930 was that they should *not* keep relatively undisturbed patients alongside the seriously ill, since the stress of this would probably make them worse:

> Moreover, the violation of the patient's rights, of which he is already conscious and which partly consists in restriction of his freedom, and partly in the fact that the attendants and medical personnel naturally and almost invariably regard him as an irresponsible person, cannot but strike further heavy blows at the weak cells. Consequently, it is necessary as quickly and as timely as possible to place such mentally diseased in the position of patients suffering from other illnesses which do not offend human dignity so manifestly. (Pavlov, 1955, p. 515)

This shows that Pavlov was not oblivious of human rights, but also that his interpretation of mental illness was always in terms of 'weak cells' or a 'weak nervous system'. As well as this idea of the nervous system being weak or strong, Pavlov believed that there were separate processes in the nervous system – of 'excitation' (causing activity) and 'inhibition' (generally suppressing bodily activity). Sleep he saw as a form of widespread inhibition; hypnotic states are also forms of inhibition and are therefore related to sleep, and 'one can hardly doubt that schizophrenia, in certain of its variations and phases, is actually a chronic hypnosis' (Pavlov, 1955, p. 514). The idea is that schizophrenics have some special weakness in cortical cells, and special states of inhibition arise as a protection against this weakness. Pavlov recommended that schizophrenics should be whispered to rather than shouted at, and generally treated gently, and this can still be regarded as a useful rule of thumb.

On the question of neurosis, rather than schizophrenia, Pavlov had more to say, since he had more data on experimentally induced neuroses. His best-known cases were accidental since they resulted from a severe flood in Leningrad in 1924. All the dogs in Pavlov's laboratory had to be made to swim from their normal quarters into the laboratory, but although at the time all of them appeared subdued by this experience, for a period after the flood some of the dogs appeared to be very disturbed, while others showed no sign of the trauma. This fitted with Pavlov's previously established view that there are pronounced individual differences between dogs' characters. Dogs 'of the inhibitable type' were put off their food by the flood more than the others. One in particular gave no salivatory reactions in its customary experimental routine, but was 'cured' if an experimenter stayed with it in the room instead of leaving it on its own, as was the usual practice. A relapse occurred two months after the flood, however, when the experimenters allowed water to trickle into the dog's experimental room and form a pool next to its stand. Not surprisingly, this reminder put the dog back into its former state of nervousness.

A second method of producing 'experimental neurosis' was to give dogs particularly difficult conditioning tasks. In most cases 'neurotic' behaviour was first observed in experiments performed for other purposes. For instance, in order to study the limits of shape perception, a dog was trained to distinguish between a circle and an elipse (when the circle was projected on a screen the dog was given food, but if an elipse was projected, there was no food). This was straightforward – very soon the dog salivated when it saw the circle, but not when it saw the elipse. But this was with a 2:1 ratio between the long and short axes of the elipse. The discrimination was gradually made more difficult. With an elipse of ratio 9:8, which looks very like a circle, the dog at first had some ability to tell it apart from a circle, but this obviously was difficult. After three weeks the dog barked when it was brought into the experimental room, squealed and struggled when it was put in the stand, and bit through all the tubes that connected the experimental stand to the observing room. This had previously been a quiet dog, and Pavlov attributed the changed behaviour to 'acute neurosis', caused by a 'clashing of excitation with inhibition', leading to 'a profound disturbance of the usual balance between these two processes'.

An alternative way of upsetting dogs is to subject them to severe electrical shocks. This would be likely to produce deleterious psychological and physical effects in any case (Seligman, 1975), but the method used in Pavlov's laboratory was to make a weak electric shock a signal for food, and then to increase its strength. Once this had been done, dogs did not perform reliably in their conditioning for several months afterwards, even for the normal stimuli of buzzers and metronomes and if given no more shocks, although in some cases bromide treatment led to a recovery (Pavlov, 1927, pp. 293–300).

Personality types

Many undergraduates become familiar with the Eysenck personality inventory – a questionnaire by which fellow students can be placed somewhere along a continuum from 'introversion' to 'extraversion'. The theory behind this system of measurement, and indeed H.J. Eysenck's theory of personality, goes back to some of Pavlov's earliest experiments on conditioned reflexes. One of the main phenomena observable in a Pavlovian conditioning stand, and one which profoundly influenced Pavlov's theories of inhibition, is that the dog in the stand falls asleep, or goes into various interesting states of drowsiness. This was at first a considerable problem, and Pavlov attempted to solve it by picking out for his experiments dogs that seemed particularly wide awake and active. He recognized a type that was 'always sniffing at everything, gazing at everything intently, and reacting quickly to the minutest sounds'. But it turned out that it was precisely this type of animal that was most likely to fall asleep in the stand, and even when let out of the stand it lay down and slept on the floor. The only way these dogs could be used in experiments was with a great variety of conditioned stimuli, with a given stimulus presented only once at a time, without long pauses when nothing happened, and with uncertainty introduced by having some negative stimuli (without food). These animals were very sociable and friendly outside the experiments and closely correspond to Eysenck's definition of an extrovert.

On the other hand a dog that appears to be a 'neurotic introvert' will probably perform very well in the conditioning stand – hence Eysenck's theory that introverts are more conditionable than extroverts. Withdrawn and 'cowardly' dogs, who cringe at the slightest outside noise, are certainly less likely to go to sleep in the conditioning stand. Pavlov had one animal referred to as a 'living instrument' and called 'Brains' because all her conditioned reflexes were extremely reliable and regular. Outside the experimental room, however, her tail was always between her legs, and she invariably shrank from human contact and so was described as of 'melancholic' temperament. Originally Pavlov assumed that the extrovert dogs were very excitable, having a predisposition to excitation in the brain – but an excess of excitation quickly brings on protective inhibition and this he supposed was why the animals tended to go to sleep. On the other hand, the introverted dogs were very 'inhibitable' but had a 'special protective mechanism' which successfully prevented this strong inhibition from spreading, and thus kept the animals awake. The reader should have no difficulty in spotting some rather tenuous stages in this reasoning: a more popular alternative is to suppose that extroverts tend to be under-aroused and thus seek maximum stimulation from the environment, whereas introverts are already over-aroused and seek to minimize external stimulation by preferring, in Pavlov's terms, 'extremely uniform conditions of life' (1927, p. 287).

Pavlov himself proposed several different schemes of personality types, but not that one. His final version was in terms mainly of 'weak' and 'strong' nervous systems, qualified by the degree of balance between the inhibitory and excitatory processes and their speed of reaction. The dog's brain could be weak or strong, and if strong, balanced or unbalanced, and if strong and balanced, quick or slow to react. There were thus four (Hippocratic) types – weak (melancholic); strong and unbalanced (choleric); strong balanced and slow (phlegmatic); and strong balanced and quick (sanguine). Pavlov took the Hippocratic temperamental types as the last word on human personality, and claimed that 'this coincidence of types in animals and human beings is convincing proof that such a systematization conforms to reality' (Pavlov, 1955, p. 482). The coincidence seems extremely forced, but the Eysenck translation into stable and unbalanced introverts and extroverts has had some successes.

The second signalling system and suggestion

The underlying theme of all Pavlov's later work was that the cerebral hemispheres function according to certain rules. These rules could be discovered, surprising as it may seem, by observing conditioned salivary reflexes in dogs, and most of the rules which apply to cerebral cortex in dogs apply also to men and women. It is because of this that Pavlov could say 'training, education and discipline of any sort are nothing but a long chain of conditioned reflexes' (1927, p. 395). However, the human species has a special character – a second kind of conditioned reflex, not available even to chimpanzees. Although the term 'reflex' implies simplicity, Pavlov's view was that the cerebral hemispheres of dogs were the site of elaborate processes of analysis and synthesis 'whose purpose is to decompose the complexity of the internal and external worlds into separate elements and moments, and then to connect all these with the manifold activity of the organism' (1955, p. 300). The reason why the conditioning method can be used is that conditioned stimuli are but examples of 'the first system of signals of reality common to men and animals'. The human species has evolved speech, which is 'a second signalling system of reality which is peculiarly ours, being the signal of the first signals' (1955, p. 262). Pavlov does not allow that speech makes all that much difference to his theory, since 'the fundamental laws governing the activity of the first signalling system must also govern that of the second, because it, too, is activity of the same nervous tissue' (1955,

p. 262). Even Gray (1979), who is very much a partisan, thinks that this is going a bit too far and that the conditioned-reflex concept is over-extended when applied to language; but the concept of a second-order signalling system for reality is better than nothing.

A curious consequence of the theory of the second signalling system is that, for Pavlov, hypnotic suggestion is more understandable than other aspects of language use since it is 'the most simple form of a typical conditioned reflex in man' (1927, p. 407). In other words the typical result of conditioning in man involves words, and in its simplest form speech may direct behaviour. Even the most complicated behaviour of chimpanzees can be interpreted as 'a combination of association and analysis', and, in Pavlov's eyes, the processes of analysis, synthesis and association that he observed in his dog experiments applied to the most complex aspects of human psychology: 'The same thing can be said of our thinking. Beyond association there is nothing more in it' (1955, p. 557).

Clearly there was nothing new in saying that human thinking is based on association – Pavlov's contribution was to tie down hypothetical processes of mental association to objective measurement in scientific experiments. The idea that mental processes can be changed by objective procedures like those used in conditioning experiments is part of the background for the development of behaviour therapy, and thus an important aspect of Pavlov's influence on psychology (Gray, 1979, chapter 7).

7

Watson's applications of behaviourism to advertising and to children

Although in his behaviourist call to arms in 1913 Watson was extremely scathing about 'pure' psychologists who were 'not interested in a psychology which concerns itself with human life', his own career switch from academic life to the hurly-burly of Madison Avenue was not altogether intentional. In one of his later books he uses as an example of 'when and how we think' the following dramatic episode:

> R's employer called him in one day and said, 'I think you would become a much more stable member of this organization if you would get married. Will you do it? I want you to answer me one way or the other before you leave this room because you either have to get married or I am going to fire you.' (Watson, 1931, p. 242)

Something not entirely unlike this had happened to Watson in October 1920. The president of Johns Hopkins University had called him in one day, and made certain remarks about Watson's personal life, with the result that Watson wrote out a brief note tendering his resignation before leaving the president's office. The problem was that Watson was having an affair with one of his research students, his wife had found love letters, and somehow or other this led to his resignation, remarriage and withdrawal from academia (Cohen, 1979). No one knows quite what happened. Tichener, the doyen of the traditional introspectionists (but, to his great credit, Watson's most loyal personal friend and supporter during the crisis), thought that things were especially sensitive at Johns Hopkins because only a few years earlier the previous head of Watson's department, Baldwin, had been forced to leave not only the university but the country after being caught with a child prostitute in a negro brothel (pausing only to hand over the editorship of the *Psychological Review* to Watson). The university was heavily dependent on the goodwill of the local and conservative financial community, and no doubt wanted to avoid further scandal. It seems unlikely that Watson was a martyr in defence of behaviourism; but quite probable that his fierce disagreement with prohibition, and his half-completed project designed to demonstrate the harmlessness of alcohol, together with his research into sexual attitudes and advocacy of greater sexual activity among students, inclined his employers, and many of his former friends and colleagues, against him.

Watson had already advocated field research, and the application of objective methods to human psychology, with the goal of finding 'general and particular methods by which behaviour may be controlled' (1914/1967, p. 11). But he cannot have anticipated doing a research project on the brands of rubber boots most favoured by the inhabitants of the banks of the Mississippi between Cairo, Illinois, and the sea. This was a temporary job in preparation for an address to the Boot Sellers League of America by the head of an advertising agency. Watson was an expert at preparing papers for conventions, and the agency head was sufficiently impressed with the work to offer him $10,000 a year for life.

Thus, by a quirk of fate, Watson the university professor became Watson the Madison Avenue executive, applying the 'laws of human behaviour' to advertising. In financial terms, this worked very well, since by 1930 Watson's salary had been increased to $70,000, 4.5 per cent of the total wage bill of J. Walter Thompson, then as now a not inconsiderable agency. In addition Watson blazed the trail in the 1920s for the popularization of the psychology of such matters as child-rearing techniques and sexual relations, commanding fees in the region of $1000 apiece for articles in magazines like *Harpers* and *Cosmopolitan.* Whether Watson should be credited with any permanent influence on advertising practice is difficult to say, but there seems little doubt that he himself was able to put his behaviourist principles to effective use in the commercial world. He spent some time lecturing Madison Avenue colleagues about the basics: 'You must never lose sight of your experimental animal – the consumer. . . . What we are struggling with is the finding of the stimulus which will produce the reaction.' And what is the reaction? 'We want the man to reach in his pocket and go down and purchase. This is the reaction.'

Watson stressed a number of other points that now seem fairly obvious. The greater the quantity of a product that the consumer uses, the more he or she will purchase, and therefore advertising should encourage intensive usage. Apparently babies less than a year old were rarely dusted with talcum powder before 1924 – Watson recommended that authorities be found to suggest that infants should be powdered from the moment of birth onwards, and as often as possible. Johnson and Johnson could encourage the use of their brand by selling the idea of purity, and suggesting that a mother who did not use their powder was less of a mother. Toothpaste should be used after every meal, not just once a day, and in this case Watson himself spoke on the radio as an eminent scientist advising listeners on the care of their teeth. Usage can be encouraged for all sorts of toiletries, and Watson early on directed the advertising for Odorono, one of the very first deodorants.

Watson made use of both the observational and the experimental techniques of his former life in arriving at recommendations. He spent two months as a counter clerk at Macy's department store in order to observe the consumer in its natural surroundings, and deduced that the position and arrangement of goods had a remarkably powerful effect on purchasing behaviour – clients were thereafter advised that placing their product by the entrance or by the cash register could in itself increase sales. But it took systematic experimentation to discover that smokers are suprisingly insensitive to the taste of their favourite brand – even after special training, Watson's subjects were unable to identify the brand of cigarettes which they smoked without being able to see from which packet they came. But this did not mean that smokers were indifferent to the identity of the cigarette; on the contrary, their 'brand loyalty' existed over and above characteristics of the product itself.

Using yet another method of investigation. Watson interviewed over a hundred potential purchasers of life insurance, and discovered that they almost all detested life-insurance salesmen. Therefore, he inferred, it was the customers' reaction to the person doing the selling, rather than to the product being sold, that would determine purchasing responses. Arthur Miller's Willie Lomax, who, in the play *Death of a Salesman* (1949), found that being 'well-liked' had turned to dust and ashes in middle age, might have attended one of Watson's lectures as a young man in the 1920s, and been told 'You are primarily selling yourself to these fellows and anything else you may be selling, any product you may be selling, is simply secondary. If you can sell yourself, you will have no trouble in selling them 12 dozen' (Cohen, 1979).

Childhood fears and neuroses

Although Watson was able to make a fortune by selling himself and his ideas to the American advertising industry, it is hard to believe that in doing so he contributed significantly to the general alleviation of human misery, even if he demonstrated that methods nurtured in the animal laboratory could be applied in the rough-and-tumble of the commercial world. His influence on behavioural methods of influencing emotions is also equivocal in some respects, since his pioneering efforts languished for several decades. But the limited experimental work he was able to perform on emotional reactions in young children supplied material which has been quoted in countless textbooks. It has recently been emphasized that Watson's experimental work with young children was not above reproach, both in terms of its statistical methodology and in terms of its kindness to the infants involved. But there is certainly no doubt of its importance in the development of psychological theories, both in behaviour therapy and in the popular imagination (Harris, 1979; Samuelson, 1980; Kazdin, 1978).

Although many more than two children were observed in the course of Watson's studies, his investigations were limited by his move into advertising, and two infants have pride of place, Little Albert and Little Peter. Watson's theoretical approach was of course to break down all emotional development into basic reactions. He thought that at birth there were only three different forms of emotional response, which would later develop into 'fear', 'rage' and 'love', these categories remaining the strongest bases for emotional appeals even in the adult consumer. Babies are most easily frightened either by very loud noises or by being dropped – both these produce startle, changes in breathing and blood circulation, and crying. Rage starts as a reaction to hampered bodily movement. Watson found that if he held a baby's legs tightly together, or pressed its arms to its sides, a variety of movements were elicited, especially in the second week after birth. The infant usually stiffens its body, may lash about with its free limbs and often holds its breath, even with its mouth open, until its face turns blue (Watson, 1931, p. 154, reassures us that 'The experiments are discontinued the moment the slightest blueness appears in the skin'). The initial reactions of 'love' in the young baby include responses that might otherwise be labelled 'affectionate' or 'good natured', such as smiling, gurgling and cooing. However, the intitial stimulus for these responses, the stroking, tickling and patting of the skin, is most effective, in Watson's view, when applied directly to 'the erogenous zones, such as the nipples, the lips and the sex organs', even in the first few months of life (Watson, 1931, p. 155).

Thus the three basics of fear, rage and love were in Watson's eyes the most instinctive human emotions, and the first to show themselves in young children; equally fundamental were the human necessities of food, shelter and sex. Even for the literate adult consumer, 'every piece of good copy must be some kind of combination of these factors', and the three emotions plus the three needs means that there are 720 combinations (Cohen, 1979, pp. 188–99). But adult emotional life is clearly more complex than combinations of infantile reactions to insecurity, constraints or tickling (although infant carry-overs are 'the general cause of unhealthy personalities'), and the main mechanism of 'how our emotional life becomes complicated' is of course the mechanism of conditioning. The child's unconditioned reactions to simple stimuli are only the starting points 'in building up those complicated habit patterns we later call our emotions' (Watson, 1931, p.

165). There is direct conditioning of emotional reactions to new stimuli, transfer of emotional effects indirectly to related sensations, and then a further level of complexity is introduced when the same stimulus (that is, often, the same person) causes fear in one situation and a little later comes to be associated with love – or rage. 'The increasing complexity brought about by these factors soon gives us an emotional organization sufficiently complicated to satisfy even the novelist and poet' (Watson, 1931, p. 165). Emotional life, normal or abnormal, was built up, Watson believed, by 'the wear and tear of the environment' taking its toll by the conditioning mechanism. As an extreme example, Watson supposed that the emotion of jealousy is not innate, or inevitable, but rather 'Jealousy is a bit of behaviour whose stimulus is a (conditioned) love stimulus the response to which is rage'. When someone sees or hears of a loved object being tampered or interfered with, we expect to observe stiffening of the whole body, reddening of the face, pronounced breathing, verbal recrimination and possibly shouting (Watson, 1931, p. 194). This is hardly an exhaustive treatment of the psychology of jealousy, but illustrates how far Watson was prepared to go in breaking down what others would consider to be natural whole units of human emotion into supposedly more primitive parts.

In the case of jealousy, Watson supposed that this only arose through conditioning experiences, instead of being innate as the Freudians insisted. To test this out he and his wife tried making love in front of their one-year-old son, without ever eliciting jealousy ('This was tested again and again': Watson, 1931, p. 191). When they instead tried fighting in front of him they got only 'behaviour of the fear type partly visually conditioned'. When this child was 2¼, Watson's second son was born, and Watson did not detect any jealousy when the older brother was taken along to watch his infant brother breast-feeding. However, by the time the older boy was 2½ he had started to attack his father, crying out 'my mama' whenever he observed Watson kissing Mrs Watson, and Watson took this to indicate that jealousy developed gradually. Many of these ideas seem weird today, and Watson's treatment of his own children is certainly not to be recommended to modern parents, but his book *The Psychological Care of the Infant and Child* was a widely used bestseller in the 1930s. Watson's general approach was much admired by Bertrand Russell, and his more extreme intentions for child rearing and the treatment of criminals made a considerable impression on Aldous Huxley, who seems to have used them for the basis of his novel *Brave New World* (1932). It was Watson's ambition, though not, as far as I know, one that was ever fulfilled, to condition the behaviour of normal infants by electric shock. ('I hope some time to try out the experiment of having a table top electrically wired in such a way that if a child reaches out for a glass or a delicate vase it will be punished, whereas if it reaches for its toys . . . it can get them without being electrically shocked': Watson, 1931, p. 185; Huxley, 1983, pp. 27–30.)

This sort of treatment would hold equally well, Watson believed, 'for adults in the field of crime'. Either people committed crimes because they were sick or they committed crimes because they were wrongly trained. In the first case the individuals concerned should be made well or, in hopeless cases, 'etherized'. On the other hand, individuals with inadequate training should be given ten to fifteen years to learn a trade and 'put on culture'. If this failed, 'they should be restrained always, and made to earn their daily bread, in vast manufacturing and agricultural institutions, escape from which is impossible. Individuals put aside thus for additional training should of course be kept in the hands of the behaviourists. . . . Naturally such a view does away completely with the criminal law . . . and with courts for the trial of criminals' (Watson, 1931, pp. 185–6).

It is hard to resist the conclusion that Watson was a Hitlerian monster but, fortunately, he was never in a position to put his more ambitious ideas into practice, and had to content himself with running his advertising accounts, and voting Republican.

The Little Albert experiment

There were two particular cases where Watson was able to gather experimental data on how conditioning experiences may alter emotional life in young children. In the first, the Little Albert experiment, fear was conditioned where none had been before. The second, the treatment of Little Peter, was one of several in which an attempt was made to remove fear and anxiety by special kinds of therapeutic experience. 'Little Albert' is the better known, partly because there are very few other reported cases of the deliberate inculcation of fear in human infants.

Albert B. weighed 21 pounds and was 11 months old when the conditioning experiment began (Watson and Rayner, 1920). He was a son of a wet nurse at a hospital for invalid children, had lived most of his life at the hospital and was selected as being exceptionally stable emotionally – 'In all the months we worked with him we never saw him cry until after our experiments were made!' (Watson, 1931, p. 159). Albert's first recorded crying occurred when he was almost 9 months old and Watson hit a 4-foot-long steel bar with a hammer just behind his head, while he was distracted by Rayner's hand waving in front of him. Even then Albert remained comparatively unmoved until this procedure had been performed for the third time. He showed no sign of emotional after-effects between then and the conditioning test five weeks later. In this, a white rat was taken out of a basket and put in front of him. As the infant reached for the rat with one hand the iron bar was struck behind his head, causing him to jump violently. Albert then reached for the rat with his other hand, the bar was banged again, and he flinched and began to whimper. He was next shown the rat a week later, when he was judged to be more tentative in reaching for it, but seemed happy to play with wooden blocks. Now the blocks were taken away, and the rat was put in front of him and the bar banged five more times, at which point it was discovered that Albert would burst into tears and crawl away from the rat at great speed without any banging. Five days later Albert was brought back and allowed to play with his blocks, which he did quite happily, but every so often the blocks were removed and replaced in turn by the rat, a rabbit, a dog, a sealskin coat, cotton wool, Watson's hair and a Santa Claus mask. He reacted negatively to all these, although not actually crying in response to Watson's hair or the cotton wool. In between these now unpleasant stimuli, Albert continued to play with his blocks, and the hair of the assistants who were tried as alternatives to Watson.

What ought to have been concluded from these results? What ought to have been concluded and what Watson did conclude are not necessarily the same thing. It is now being said that Watson should not have concluded anything at all from an experiment on just one child, that Little Albert might have developed an aversion to rats and rabbits even if there had been no enormous iron bar being clanged, and so on and so forth (Harris, 1979; Samuelson, 1980). For present purposes, our interest is in the theory that the data were used to support, and not in the reliability of the data. But the reader whould note two points about the Little Albert experiment. First it supports a general belief that infants, even of less than 1 year of age, are not indifferent to their experiences – the child is father to the man – and that nasty experiences, especially, may have peculiar after-effects. But second, the Little Albert experiment certain does not prove, as Watson sometimes implied, that *everything* which happens to an infant has long-lasting effects, or that all the phenomena observable in infants correspond exactly to the descriptions of the dog's salivatory reflexes given by Pavlov. In fact, conditioning procedures used with infants less than a year old are not always reliable, although certain standard results, such as anticipatory mouthing at the sight of a feeding bottle, leave little doubt that normal life is producing conditioned effects.

A more benign technique of demonstrating simple conditioning in an infant at about Albert's age is to clap one's hands several times over its eyes. This should at first produce blinking in response only to the clap, but after four or five responses the infant should close its eyes if the hands are moved, but stopped just short of a clap (see the chapter on 'Conditioned reflexes' in Pieper, 1963, which begins with the proverb 'A burnt child dreads the fire'). It seems fairly safe to conclude that Little Albert became distressed by the sight of both the rat and the Santa Claus mask because of the experience of being made to jump out of his skin when the rat was previously presented. In Watson's hands this became a 'prolific goose for laying golden eggs' since it provided him, he thought, with 'an explanatory principle that will account for the enormous complexity in the emotional behaviour of adults' (Watson, 1931, p. 161). In my view it would be foolish to claim that experiences as extreme as those suffered by Albert are not likely to have some carry-over effects in infants, but even more ridiculous to assume that conditioning is a sufficient explanation for all adult emotions.

The Little Peter treatment

The original plan had been to remove the conditioned emotional responses from Albert before they became chronic, but this was never carried out (either because of the removal of Albert from the hospital, when he was adopted, or because of the removal of Watson from Johns Hopkins University). Watson speculated that Albert might still have a phobia for sealskin coats when he grew up, and that Freudian psychotherapists might try to cure him by providing him with the insight that his fear of coats was caused by his having been scolded for attempting to play with his mother's pubic hair in the Oedipal phase. It was Watson's own view that unpleasant early experiences associated with maternal pubic hair might indeed produce a conditioned fear response which could be 'transferred' to fur coats in adult life, and that one of the distinctive things about such internal emotions is that '*We have never learned to talk about them*' (Watson, 1931, p. 166, original italics).

But partly, I think, because most of his experimental work was done with young children, Watson did not set much store by talking as a method of therapy, and recommended instead more direct methods of treatment. Had Albert continued under Watson's care, he was due to be exposed to several methods designed to make his fear of rats, rabbits and sealskin disappear. These included constant confrontation with the feared stimuli, the encouragement of manipulation of the feared object by the experimenter setting an example or by the experimenter taking the child's hand and forcing it to touch the rat, and the 'reconditioning' method. The reconditioning was to take the form of presenting the original stimulus (the rat) but calling forth different emotional responses, either by tactile stimulation of the child's lips, nipples and genitals, or by giving the child food.

After Watson was settled in New York, and working full time on Madison Avenue, he obtained a research grant to continue work on the emotional life of children, and supervised the efforts of Mary Cover Jones (1924a, 1924b, 1974) to alleviate specific fears in children living in a charitable institution. Most of the children studied by Mary Cover Jones were under 5. The ones she was interested in were those who cried and trembled (the fear response) when an animal, such as a frog, rat or rabbit, was shown to them. Individual children often had individual fears, but a jumping frog was the animal most likely to frighten these urban under-5s. Various methods of curing these fears were tried. Simply giving repeated presentations of the same animal, in the hope that familiarity would breed contempt (the method of disuse) led usually to repeated tears. A 5-year-old girl afraid of rabbits was given a daily dose of pictures of friendly rabbits, plasticine toy rabbits and pleasant rabbit stories. This had the desired effect in so far as the child happily talked about rabbits, and even claimed 'I touched your rabbit and stroked it and never cried' (this was not true, but might count today as positive cognitive restructuring). However, when the real rabbit was brought in, she sobbed for it to be taken away, as she had done before. Thus the 'method of verbal organization' was discounted. Jones herself was inclined to recommend social methods of treatment (1924b). Small boys afraid of rabbits on their own sometimes developed an interest if shown rabbits in the company of small girls who liked rabbits. Vicarious social learning of this sort has been much studied more recently by Bandura (1973). However, Watson himself was distrustful of the social methods, partly because they could go wrong. Occasionally the social companions, who were supposed to be merely setting a good example, would turn on the infant patient. Little Arthur, afraid of frogs, was not helped when his friends picked up a frog and chased him with it; he screamed and fled. This, Watson said, was liable to breed more negative reactions, not just to the animal, but to human society as a whole. Also, at this young age there was the possibility of social transmission of the phobia – sometimes well-balanced infants, whose presence was supposed to reassure their friend who was afraid of rabbits, themselves joined in the crying.

Watson was much more in favour of 'direct conditioning' as used to treat Little Peter. This child was active and eager, at 3 years of age, and judged to be well adjusted, apart from the fact that he was extremely afraid of rats, rabbits, fur coats, feathers, cotton wool, frogs and fish. From this list, Watson said 'one might well think that Peter was merely Albert B grown up', but of course the source of Peter's fear was unknown. Initially Peter fell flat on his back in a paroxysm of fear when a white rat was dropped into his playpen. Then, after a two-month stay in hospital with scarlet fever, he was attacked by a large dog when getting into a taxi to go home. After this all his fears became even worse and the method of direct unconditioning was then begun. It started with the display of a rabbit in a wire cage while Peter was eating his mid-afternoon lunch and ended, forty sessions later, with Peter eating his lunch with one hand while fondling the rabbit in his lap with the other.

The idea behind the method was that there was a gradual scale of closeness to the fear-provoking stimulus, and that the positive emotions aroused by eating lunch should allow a progression up this scale until even intimate contact with the rabbit took on some of the pleasant associations. The scale had seventeen steps – at first the rabbit was in its cage, which was brought closer and closer each day; then it was free in the room; and eventually it sat on the lunch tray. Six different observers independently rated Peter's adjustment to the various stages, and it was quite clear that his emotions underwent genuine change. We cannot be so sure about the reasons for these changes. Watson felt they were the direct result of the enjoyment of eating, and that the method would have been even more successful if Peter had been hungrier, or if he had been 'stroked, petted and rocked' in order to counteract his fears with sexual feelings. Mary Cover Jones, who performed the therapy, laid more emphasis on social factors of encouragement and imitation. Peter made his most striking advances after particular social incidents. In one case watching another child hold the rabbit led to imitation, and the most dramatic improvement of all occurred after a Dr S, who was a particular favourite of Peter's, had come along to watch. Peter insisted on calling Dr S 'my papa', which suggests a somewhat more complex form of emotional support than digestive contentment. A more straightforward factor was at work when Peter subsequently underwent a relapse, since the relapse occurred just after Peter had suffered a scratch when he was at the stage of helping the experimenter put the rabbit back in its cage. But, this setback was only temporary, and after another dozen lunch sessions, Peter was showing what Jones took to be genuine fondness for the rabbit, was heard to say 'I like the rabbit', and allowed it to nibble at his fingers.

There are thus good grounds for claiming that these studies of the Heckscher Foundation children, published by Jones but initiated and supervised by Watson, are the first case histories of behaviour therapy, and the first successes (as well as the first failures) of the application of learning theory to clinical problems. Watson was a wayward and peculiar man, and the swashbuckling success of his behaviourist methods in advertising cigarettes and baby powder may have owed more to his physical resemblance to

Errol Flynn than to the soundness of his psychological principles. But the Heckscher studies anticipated both the method of *in vivo* desensitization and many later analyses of social learning in children, which are still in use as reliable and safe procedures for the relief of anxiety (Kazdin, 1978).

8

Applications of stimulus-response theories from Thorndike to Wolpe

Thorndike's first experiments were designed to prove that cats and dogs act by conditioned impulses, rather than by using memory or anticipation (1898; pp. 7–10 above). In his next monograph (1901), Thorndike went on to claim that this was also true of monkeys: 'In their method of learning, the monkeys do not advance far beyond the generalized mammalian type.' To Thorndike's eye, there was no evidence of imitation, accurate discrimination, or memory in the behaviour of monkeys; they simply formed associations faster than other mammals. One might go on from this assumption to deduce that human learning must take an entirely different course. But already, in 1898, Thorndike was saying about his principle of stimulus-response connections that 'this hitherto unsuspected law of animal mind may prevail in human mind to an extent hitherto unknown' (Thorndike, 1898, p. 105). In fact, soon after doing his first work with animals, Thorndike became professor of educational psychology at the Teachers College of Columbia University and concerned himself mainly with human abilities. But this closer contact with research on human beings did not make him change his mind – in 1931 he still felt that the stimulus-response principle could be applied to human activities, and in his book *Human Learning* (1931) he said 'the situation-response formula is adequate to cover learning of any sort, whether it comes with ideas or without, conscious or unconscious, impulsive or deliberate, by *Gestalten* or even by a miracle' (p. 132).

Many students are still familiar with one of Thorndike's particular contributions to education, which may be used to illustrate both the virtues and vices of his general approach. Perhaps Thorndike's most frequently read publication is *The Teacher's Word Book of 20,000 Words*, expanded to include 30,000 words (Thorndike and Lorge, 1944). If language is composed of word habits, and habits are accumulations of practice, then it is useful to know exactly how often any given word is used. The first two chapters of Thorndike's *Human Learning* are about the 'frequency of a situation' and the 'frequency of a connection' – frequency or how often something happens was the fundamental variable in Thorndike's theory. Thus he developed the variable of word frequency – how often we are likely to come across a particular word in a standard set of sources – and Thorndike actually counted up frequency values for the 20,000 most commonly used words.

There are surely virtues in measurement, or at least utilities in measurement, and that is why the Thorndike–Lorge word-frequency list is still consulted for experiments on words. But there may be vices too in measurement, or if not in measurement, in excessive quantification and systematization applied to human learning. Thorndike's first educational recommendation was that mechanical repetition should be the primary tool of the teacher – 'the only way to teach fractions in algebra, for example, is to get the pupil to do, do, do' (Thorndike, 1898, p. 105). This is quite the opposite of the stress on insight, understanding and personal discovery which characterizes more enlightened approaches to education. There are now perhaps some who feel that Thorndike was right all along, and that drilling pupils in the three R's, with objective and quantitative tests to assess what pupils can actually do, would be preferable to enlightenment that produces no visible positive results. But those who are against too much 'pre-digestion' of material, especially in textbooks, and against too many 'paragraph headings, and cross-references, and examination questions', would probably be against Thorndike. William James, whose massive two-volume *The Principles of Psychology* has just been reprinted, partly on the grounds of its literary merit, was very much against paragraph headings and numbered exercises, 'and every other up-to-date device for frustrating the natural movement of the mind when reading', because he believed that such interruptions would prevent 'that irresponsible rumination of the material in one's own way which is the soul of culture'. This quotation is from the introduction that James wrote to Thorndike's *The Elements of Psychology*. Although, as Thorndike's mentor and friend, James was recommending the book, it did itself contain many numbered exercises, paragraph headings, and questions and directions in small print, and James's comments are rather back-handed. Could it be, he wondered, that Thorndike had become 'a high-priest of the American text-book Moloch, in whose belly living children's minds are turned to ashes'? Nevertheless, the eminent James gave Thorndike's book a hearty recommendation, and although James's own book has become a classic, it is a classic partly as the last in its line. In practice paragraph headings, and cross-references, with easily digested outlined boxes of material, form part of the established religion of textbook writers, and Thorndike may be regarded as one of the founding fathers of this tradition.

Tolman's purposive behaviourism in animals and men

Regrettably, Tolman's purposive behaviourism is an example of the inverse plausibility rule for psychological theories. This states that, by and large, the practical effects of a psychological theory are in inverse proportion to its general soundness and plausibility. Thus a bizarre and astounding dogma, such as Freud's contention that *all* human motivation and thought are dominated by sex, may come to be fervently accepted by thousands, and Watson's behaviourism, which Tolman rightly derided for its inherently unsound dependence on muscle twitches as substitutes for thoughts, has had far more influence on clinical and educational psychology than Tolman's more sensible and considered reflections on how rats negotiate mazes. Tolman liked the Gestalt field theories about human personality put forward by Lewin (e.g.

1935), and occasionally concerned himself with repression and unconscious motivation, but there was not very much direct application of his theory to human affairs in his lifetime.

One should mention, however, that Tolman attempted to contribute to the solution of what is now perhaps the single biggest human problem in his book *Drives Towards War* (1942). Brought up as a Quaker pacifist, Tolman was appalled by all war, but recognized and tried to analyse human motives which favoured war, even as a 'glorious human adventure'. He used his learning theory in starting from biological drives, which he supposed supplied the first and most basic human needs. For Tolman the basics included curiosity, play and aesthetic experiences as well as hunger, thirst and sex. In order to satisfy these initial drives, individuals learn certain useful techniques, including 'money-getting' and social skills, and these techniques are either 'self-assertive' or 'collective'. A child who develops self-assertive techniques tends to become 'bumptious and demanding' and eventually runs into resistance from a parental figure or from superiors in social or educational pecking orders. If the child then identifies with the parental figure this should generally lead to socially approved behaviours. Often, however, 'self-abasive' techniques are learned in order to conform to social pressures, with concomitant repressed hostility towards parental figures and other frustrating agents. It is this dammed-up hostility which interacts with the collective technique of identifying with the group, and becomes converted into hostile feelings towards outsiders – 'This is the set-up in what I would call *neurotically motivated war*' (Tolman, 1942, p. 86). Relatively benign loyalties to the group lead to equally powerful hostile feelings against any attacking enemies.

This is clearly an *ad hoc* and inconsistent analysis, but Tolman's conclusion is still worthy of consideration: 'A war in response to outside aggression does tend to preserve in some measure the communal life of a nation (if God and oil be on her side); but only in some measure. The accompanying losses are today obviously all too great' (Tolman, 1942, p. 92). In order to save the world from its horrors Tolman proposes a 'workable myth' of psychological adjustment, composed of six principles, which boil down to three practical devices: (1) an economic order which minimizes biological frustrations in all individuals; this could be obtained by a compromise between self-assertive private initiative and collective means – Tolman imagines 'something like state socialism' being necessary; (2) to avoid repression and neurosis, children will have to be helped to identify with and copy appropriate adults – Tolman believed that as much damage was done by children trying to be like their parents, as by their trying to be unlike their parents; and (3) to avoid wars, there should be a World Federation, with its own handsome and commanding buildings, its own flag and its own world anthem. Tolman says he will be more loyal to this than to the United States, and individuals all over the world should identify with this supranational group. This last did not commend Tolman to the authorities when explicit oaths of loyalty were demanded of university staff in California in the early 1950s, and, as he said himself, the whole idea is a utopian dream, with little chance of success. In some ways Tolman's Utopia is repressive, since he wants photographs of the World Federation buildings in every home and, apart from fighting the common enemies represented by disease and earthquakes, he imagines that the youth of the future will unite to put down 'rebellious subgroups which seek to break away'. But in general Tolman opposed discrimination against minorities. The argument from his theory was that cognitive maps represent reason, and that broad and comprehensive cognitive maps will represent the triumph of rationality over emotionally disordered hates and fears. By analogy with the intelligent performances of his rats in mazes, Tolman hopes that eventually people will be able to

> learn to look before and after, learn to see that there are often round-about and safer paths to their quite proper goals – learn, that is, to realize that the well-beings of White and of Negro, of Catholic and of Protestant, of Christian and of Jew, of American and of Russian (and even of males and females) are mutually interdependent. (Tolman 1948, p. 208)

Practical techniques from Hullian postulates

It is, most unfortunately, a characteristic of appeals to reason that they utterly fail to overcome either emotional prejudices or neurotic habits. Even if it is not a question of high-level rationality, but just a matter of seeking obvious goals, then human goal-seeking mechanisms are fallible. Children do not stop wetting the bed just because they would prefer to have a dry bed; adult agoraphobics do not lose their fear of leaving the house just because they decide they would like a holiday; and desires for peace have never yet stopped wars. Hull's theory of drives and habits undoubtedly had more initial influence on clinical psychology than Tolman's cognitive theory (although, as we shall see, current 'cognitive behaviour modification' is getting very Tolmanian). This was partly because Hull put forward laws which he and others believed were even more fundamental than goal-seeking. Hull himself wanted to provide, not practical techniques, but an all-embracing set of theoretical principles:

> As suggested by the title, this book attempts to present in an objective, systematic manner the primary, or fundamental, molar principles of behaviour. . . . Consequently the present work may be regarded as a general introduction to the theory of all the behavioural (social) sciences. (Hull, 1943, p. *v*)

This could be put up for the award of Most Grandiose Preface to any Book in Psychology, especially since the book is mainly about experiments on laboratory rats. It is true that the first professor of sociology in England, L.T. Hobhouse of the London School of Economics, started his career with a book about animal learning, called *Mind in Evolution* (1901), and went on from there; but by 1943 it was a bit much to expect the same book to serve as an introduction to all the social sciences, even theoretically. The remarkable thing was that not only was Hull's theory popular with those conducting the laboratory experiments (in the 1940s 70 per cent of the papers in relevant journals referred to it), but it seemed to serve as a useful stimulus for fellow members of the Yale Institute of Human Relations, and for others interested in social and clinical problems. The emphasis on drives in Hull's theory in fact allowed Hullians such as Neal Miller and O.H. Mowrer to take over many Freudian ideas about frustrations and conflicts and consequent displacements and repressions. But the most lasting memorials to Hull's optimism may be two simple and practical techniques for dealing with superficial but troubling problems. In neither case can it be said that Hull's equations are being applied, but the general ideas of applying fundamental laws by altering 'conditions under which habits are set up and function' are clearly at work.

In the first instance, the 'bell and pad' treatment of bedwetting, the incentive for a new method arose when O.H. Mowrer and his wife had responsibilities in one of the residential cottages for disturbed children run by the Yale Institute (Mowrer, 1980). About half the children were chronically enuretic – it is certainly true that anxiety, emotional disturbance or unhappiness is associated with this symptom, but how or why remains obscure. Punishments, even of the most vile kind, have little effect, perhaps partly because they increase anxiety. Benign exhortations and inducements are similarly almost worthless. Conditioning techniques designed directly to establish a habit of waking up in response to internal pressures have, by contrast, a well-established record of success. The very first attempts made by Mowrer, unpublished at the time, required a trick bed, which collapsed on one side, rolling out the unfortunate occupant, when wetness was electrically detected. It was then discovered that a loud electric bell, placed in a metal box, was equally effective as a wakening agent, and the moisture detecting pad, connected to a bell, is still in use. Any electrical apparatus is daunting to some, and the use of the bell and pad requires effort on the part of adult supervisors, who must wake up too, but children whose urinary habits are retrained by these means suffer no adverse side-effects, and indeed are often made happier by the release from the shame and ignominy of their complaint.

The theories and methods of Wolpe

Urinating in one's sleep is a very specific behavioural problem, even if not unrelated to general emotional insecurities, and the bell and pad (more accurately, pad and bell) treatment could not, I think, be applied to any other syndrome. The only other behavioural trick which approaches the pad and bell method in the reliability of its effects is the method of 'systematic desensitization' developed by Wolpe (1958), which has a very much wider range of application. There is no doubt that Wolpe was deeply influenced by the Hullian school of thought, even though geographically distant, in South Africa, when he performed his first research and therapy. Wolpe's credo is reminiscent of Hull's preface in its lawfulness: 'Everything in this book rests on the fundamental assumption that the behaviour of organisms, including human beings, conforms to causal laws just as other phenomena do' (Wolpe, 1976, p. 3). And this was more than lip-service, as experiments on cats preceded the first human patients. Wolpe's theories were in a sense even more mechanistic than Hull's, since they referred to principles of the nervous system: the name 'reciprocal inhibition' was taken by Wolpe from Sherrington's work on the spinal cord. In essence, reciprocal inhibition is a more carefully worked-out version of Watson's 'direct conditioning', and 'systematic desensitization' is a way of applying the Little Peter treatment (see pp. 88–91) to neurotic adults.

Wolpe's substitute for both Little Peter and Little Albert was Septima, a short-haired tabby cat, with white throat and paws, who was the seventh cat tested among twelve that all showed roughly similar effects (Wolpe, 1952, 1976). It is possible to define neurotic behaviour in such a way that almost any cat given an electric shock in an experimental cage becomes neurotic. If a cat has been put in the special cage once or twice and given a series of shocks, then, reasonably enough, it will strongly resist being put back into that cage a week later. Once forced inside, its eyes will dilate with fear, it may mew, howl or scratch, and perhaps raise its fur. The 'neurotic' aspect of this is that (1) the fear tends not to diminish with time: even when put back several times without any shocks, or when put back months after being shocked, the animal may seem just as afraid; and (2) the cat refuses to eat in the cage, even when it has been without food for days, whether or not it has been used to eating in the cage before its trauma. (It should be said that this sort of experiment is rarely performed nowadays and is certainly not performed in the United Kingdom; and that since the experiments with these twelve cats, Wolpe has devoted himself to relieving the misery of large numbers of unacceptably anxious human beings.)

The refusal to eat is 'maladaptive' in the sense that the animals gain nothing by it, and their fears seem excessive. However, since such behaviour is characteristic of all cats (and dogs) tested in this way, and is common in wild animals when they are caught and confined, even if without any pain or discomfort, then we must presume that it is part of the animal's 'normal' rather than abnormal psychology. Wild animals, greedy enough to start eating in circumstances even remotely dangerous, may pay for their relaxation with their lives. Natural selection thus puts a premium on wariness and jumpiness rather than imperturbability, and this is probably the reason why 'anxiety' is the big problem in clinical psychology, and relatively few human individuals go to their doctor to complain that they are too relaxed. This evolutionary interpretation would add weight to analogies drawn between over-anxious cats and over-anxious people – what ways are there to cheat our personal and evolutionary histories, and lower anxiety levels to where we want them?

Wolpe found that the Little Peter treatment worked well with his cats. The cats would initially not eat even outside the cage in the room where they had been shocked. But if they were taken into another room, slightly different in appearance from the original, and were able to feed comfortably, then their anxiety seemed to be reduced even when they were taken back to the scene of their original trauma. This is the same idea, of gradual reconditioning, that was used in getting Little Peter to eat, first with his feared white rabbit a long distance away, and then with the rabbit progressively closer. It was not necessarily a very rapid or easy process though. Septima was made neurotic by being shocked on 21 and 23 August 1947, and, after almost daily therapeutic and testing sessions, did not begin to eat comfortably in the experimental room until 16 October: it took until 25 June 1948 for her to be declared cured, on the criteria that she had become indifferent to the hooter which had originally been sounded to signal the electric shocks, and purred and ate her food pellets even when the hooter was on.

The therapeutic process for Septima involved three different rooms, apart from the one she was originally shocked in, and a gradual change from eating in conditions remote from those which aroused fear to eating in the exact place where the experimental traumas had occurred. Other cats recovered more quickly – some simply when food was presented by a familiar human hand instead of being dropped down a shute, even in the shock cage. Wolpe noted that Septima was much calmer when accompanied by a friendly laboratory assistant, who had not been involved in the shocking procedure, than by himself, and of course it is usually the case that nervous cats respond well to being gently stroked.

In Wolpe's theoretical scheme, *anything* which acts as an anti-anxiety agent can be useful, as long as this anti-anxiety state can be conditioned to the same stimulus that causes the problem. In applying this principle (of reciprocal inhibition) to human patients, the most generally applicable antidote for anxiety is muscular relaxation. However Wolpe also often used a variety of alternatives under the heading of 'assertion', which included getting people to stand up for themselves against domineering relatives and colleagues, and also 'outward expression of friendly, affectionate, and other non-anxious feelings' (Wolpe, 1958, p. 114).

When Wolpe received the 1979 Distinguished Scientific Award for the Application of Psychology at the American Psychological Association meeting in 1980, he reiterated his belief that the future of psychotherapy should lie with methods 'founded on principles of learning established in the psychological laboratory' (Wolpe, 1981, p. 159), if only we would give up leaving patients 'interminably in chancery' in futile psychoanalysis, and train more people with Wolpe's methods instead of Freud's methods. Expensive therapy lasting for many years, with no change at all in the patient's initial complaint, is not at all unusual in psychoanalysis, and so it is hardly surprising that those who have a scientific belief in the method of learning from experience feel that there is room for improvement.

Wolpe's own line of treatment is based on a series of interviews between himself and individual patients. Having been a convinced Freudian before being converted to Hullian enlightenment, it is arguable that Wolpe's own success may be due to his combining the catharsis of emotional confession with active emotional re-training, with Wolpe himself playing the parts of both confessor and coach. It is a subjective problem which usually drives the neurotic to seek treatment, and for Wolpe 'the patient's story is the primary data' (1981, p. 162). Patients first describe in detail this history, in so far as they know it, of their complaints and also give the background history of their childhood memories, educational record and sexual relations, whether it is immediately relevant or not. In mild cases, of course, just talking over one's troubles with a reassuring expert can be a considerable relief (and 'inadvertent deconditioning of unadaptive anxiety responses may take place': Wolpe, 1978, p. 442; 1958, p. 193). But not all neuroses are so mild. Some idea of the severity of a patient's neurosis (but by no means an exact measure) can be obtained by questionnaires. The one Wolpe used originally had questions such as 'Are you afraid of falling when you are on a high place?' 'Are your feelings easily hurt?' 'Do you keep in the background on social occasions?' and so on, with answers to be given on a 5-point scale, varying from 'never', to 'practically always'. Someone who gives the 'always' answer to a range of questions like this must be pretty miserable, and a downward shift in the total score can be used as a measure of the patient's progress in therapy. The sorts of human problems that Wolpe felt he was able to solve were given as case histories (1958, *passim*).

Mr W: insecurity countered by assertion

Mr W was a commercial traveller with an unhappy childhood and an unfaithful wife. He had a guilty habit of staring at buxom women and pervasive social anxieties and feelings of insecurity. He had very strong feelings about the iniquities of racial discrimination, which for a commercial traveller in South Africa was unusual as well as unsettling. By the fourth interview, when all these things had been discussed, Wolpe 'attempted to give Mr W a perspective' by noting that he had always been a rather anxious person, and was no doubt suffering further from the feeling that his wife had never loved him. However, he needed in the first place to get over his deficiencies in the social sphere by expressing his views as clearly and as forcefully as possible no matter how critical his colleagues and friends might seem to be of him. In a nutshell, the therapist's advice was 'Stop being on the defensive and stop apologizing for yourself' (Wolpe, 1958, p. 124). At the fifth interview Mr W reported that he still felt tense in company, but had been buoyed up by the experience of asserting himself among fellow commercial travellers in the bar lounge of a hotel. Wolpe then suggested that now was the time for Mr W to go home and express his true feelings to his wife, whose infidelities he had previously condoned. Mr W immediately went home and told his wife that her extramarital relationship had got to stop, to which she replied, 'It's about time. You're jealous at last.' Mr W was thus feeling much improved by the sixth interview but was still troubled by insomnia. Wolpe hypnotized him into a deep trance and suggested that he would feel much more relaxed in future. By the ninth interview, which was just over a year since the treatment had begun, Mr W reported that he was socially in demand and getting a kick out of life, having started to tell jokes at parties, joined a lodge and taken up public speaking. His fantasies about very buxom women continued, but with much less guilt. At a follow-up session two years later (without any intervening pep talks) Mr W regarded himself as a happy man. People continued to remark on how much he had changed, and his wife, who had not previously taken part in the therapy, announced to Wolpe that her husband had become a pleasure to live with.

This case indicates the directive nature of Wolpe's method; his piecemeal treatment of individual symptoms, and his initial inclination towards hypnosis (also the subject of a book by Hull, 1933).

Mr V: countering sexual anxieties

Mr V was a 40-year-old architect who was good at his work, and without general anxieties, but who complained of premature ejaculations. Having had only intermittent and casual sexual relationships in his twenties, he had developed severe sexual difficulties in his thirties after a period of long abstinence. He had now met a woman he wanted to marry and had sought professional help before attempting intercourse with her. After three exploratory interviews, Wolpe explained his theory (which was not exactly original) that anxiety provoked by the occasion of sexual intercourse could interfere with male physiology to the extent of eliciting premature ejaculation, and that anxiety could be countered by relaxation as a first step, and by increasing familiarity with the circumstances of intercourse in the absence of the stresses and excitements of the act itself. For six interviews over four weeks Wolpe trained Mr V in muscular relaxation, at the same time as building up his confidence by telling him of success in similar cases and preparing him for difficulties by arguing that even complete failure at the first two or three attempts at intercourse is no reason why a couple should not eventually find sexual happiness. Then Wolpe sent Mr V away; he was not to come back until he had explained his problems to Anne, his intended. Mr V came back in a month, but with only failure to report. He had persuaded Anne to attempt intercourse, but had been too nervous at the first attempt, and after that had lost all sexual feeling and did not even get an erection.

Wolpe's advice was that it was far too early for sexual intercourse, and over the next few weeks Mr V was instructed on no account to attempt it, but to try to enjoy other physical intimacies for their own sake. Under instructions Mr V first lay naked in bed with Anne with no other activities to follow and found that erections returned; the next step was the handling of his erect penis by Anne without any ejaculation; only after several nights of this was intercourse attempted. There were some setbacks, but even after the first ninety-second insertion Mr V understandably began to feel much happier about his chances, and a seaside holiday with Anne appeared to have a very liberating effect. Eight months later Mr V reported that he and Anne were happily married and that all his sexual problems had disappeared.

Here there was an overt sexual problem – apparently unrelated to any other difficulties. In contrast to the Freudian tradition, in which nothing is ever what it seems, Wolpe treats the superficial problem directly. The relation of anxiety to many sexual problems is very direct – it either causes them in the first place or else makes them worse. And the importance that may be attached to sexual performance, as well as its arousing and exciting nature, can itself start off anxiety, so it is possible for vicious circles of fear to change mild apprehension into sexual nullity. Direct therapy for these sorts of problems is now (and perhaps always has been) almost a profession in itself, but Wolpe deserves some of the credit for the 'go slow' technique of the intercourse ban as well as the direct attack on anxiety by muscular relaxation and friendly reassurance. It is a strange irony that direct non-Freudian methods of therapy seem to have their greatest appeal as treatments for the most fundamentally Freudian conditions – those which frustrate the great sexual drive of the id.

Miss T: desensitization to social stimuli

The procedure for which Wolpe is best known is 'systematic desensitization'. This involves deconditioning anxiety by a little-by-little method, when the anxiety is irrationally evoked by a set of specific problems or outside stimuli. Wolpe was particularly keen on the method of using deep muscular relaxation to antagonize anxiety. Anxiety usually involves being tense – in peripheral musculature as well as inner feeling. Thus not many anxious patients are capable of learning to relax completely in the face of their real-life fears. But many can produce very relaxed muscles during the therapeutic interview, especially with the aid of drugs or hypnosis, at the same time as *imagining* some moderately difficult situations. In learning the relaxation technique over a number of weeks, patients first grip the arm of their chair, then completely relax their hands, to notice the difference. Then particular muscles – arm, forehead, jaw, neck, shoulder and so on – are deliberately relaxed in turn. With practice, patients could then keep fairly relaxed when Wolpe told them to.

Miss T was a 46-year-old dressmaker with peptic ulcers. Almost any social interaction made her nervous, and almost any nervousness made her nauseous. She had been happy at home but slow at school, and she left school at 14 to help her mother at home. There she attracted little attention from young men, and she came to feel inferior and nervous in male company. When, eventually, at 33, she had her first and only affair, she became fond of her lover, and was deeply hurt as after four years of their association he went away on business and came back engaged to someone else. It is hardly surprising that she was unable to respond to Wolpe's first instructions to assert herself more and stand up to other people. Since this did not work, Wolpe began to train Miss T in the techniques of muscular relaxation, and at the same time constructed with her a 'Hierarchy on the theme of her sensitivity to people' (Wolpe, 1958, p. 149). This was a list of circumstances the contemplation of which made Miss T increasingly nervous as she went up the list. At the bottom was 'Being at a party with other girls who work with her'; in the middle was 'Going up to receive a prize at the end-of-the-year party'; and at the top was 'Having an interview with any doctor or lawyer' (there were thirteen items altogether, not all needed at the same time).

When the hierarchy of circumstances had been agreed on, and Miss T had been trained to relax, 6 sessions took place in the following month, with 2 or 3 sessions per month for the next three months. Miss T was both hypnotized and relaxed while Wolpe narrated to her one or more scenes from the hierarchy, moving up through the list as the sessions progressed, the patient being supposed to visualize to herself the occasion being described while remaining as relaxed as possible. A party with other girls from work was imagined without undue disturbance at the first session. Telling her employer she had done incorrect stitching because of someone else's wrong instructions went off (in fantasy) during hypnosis at the third session with only slight associations of anxiety reported by Miss T on waking from her trance. Items higher up the list were usually disturbing when first presented under these conditions, but repetitions of the items succeeded in producing diminished reactions during the therapeutic sessions. And by the eighth session even the first presentation of the third most difficult scene, 'Being phoned by a man to whom recently introduced', produced hardly any anxiety. However, the first presentation of scene 2, 'Unexpectedly finding a strange man when visiting her brother's house', created a stir at the eleventh session, and was still disturbing after five imaginary repetitions during this session. Following this there was also an external setback when Miss T was shouted at by a supervisor at work. In any event she was now feeling continuously nervous, with a characteristic sick feeling in her stomach.

Continuous and pervasive feelings of anxiety are difficult to treat except by drugs, but Wolpe found that occasionally dramatic and immediate relief occurred after patients inhaled a gas mixture (70 per cent carbon dioxide and 30 per cent oxygen) which briefly produces a stupor, with lights flashing before the eyes, tingling sensations and sometimes loss of consciousness. Perhaps this interrupts a vicious circle of symptoms connected with respiration, since an initial anxiety attack may produce hyperventilation (too much breathing), which in turn leads to lightheadedness, dizziness and feelings of unreality, as well as numbness and tremors, pains in muscles, and in particular pain in the heart. Any or some of these secondary symptoms might themselves cause anxiety, or according to Wolpe's theory might be very suitable stimuli for conditioned associations with the original anxiety-provoking event.

Miss T was given the carbon dioxide and oxygen treatment, and immediately said she felt better. Then the desensitization sessions continued, but with the addition of scenes involving shouting. After another five sessions Miss T was able to visualize without any nervousness even her worst fears (which now included men punching each other with Miss T as the only witness, as well as the 'strange man in brother's house' scene and the doctor's interviews). The crucial point of course is whether this made any difference when she was not being hypnotized in Wolpe's office. In fact Miss T appears to have become emotionally imperturbable to a slightly worrying degree. Her questionnaire scores now indicated little social anxiety, and she found herself happily talking to other guests when she went away on holiday to a hotel by herself. On returning home she had to deal with her mother having a heart attack in the middle of the night, but this did not upset her in the least. Whether this sort of impassivity is a good thing or not is debatable, but at least Miss T's ulcers cleared up, and her physician reported a year after Wolpe's therapy that she had remained in good condition medically.

Wolpe's methods of behaviour therapy – conclusions

Although in 1981 Wolpe bemoaned the lack of impact of his kind of 'behaviour analysis' in North America, all the psychological methods of anxiety-reduction which he put forward in 1958 have received a certain amount of attention, from clinical psychologists if not from psychiatrists. In particular, the three methods used in the case histories I have just repeated – of encouraging patients to assert themselves and to stand up to people who make them anxious in their everyday life; of step-by-step, matter-of-fact progress in sexual activities, under the guidance of a therapist, as a means of overcoming sexual anxieties; and of systematic desensitization during a series of interviews, by getting the patient to work through a list of scenes which are particular sources of anxiety, while at the same time remaining relaxed – all of these individual methods have been widely adopted by others, even if those others do not always adopt Wolpe's more general background technique of analysing the personal history of each individual patient. Wolpe was also able to claim, in 1978, that in his early work he had anticipated the later trend of emphasizing the alteration of a patient's thought processes during therapy.

Although it would be unwise to accept Wolpe's work as a complete theory without flaws, or as the last word on therapeutic techniques, he deserves credit as a humane and creative pioneer in the search for psychological techniques of combating irrational anxieties. To quote from his citation in the *American Psychologist* (American Psychological Association, 1980, p. 44):

He played a vital role in developing the theory and practice of behavior therapy, currently one of the most widely employed of therapeutic procedures. Wolpe's therapeutic methods, especially desensitization, have been successfully used to reduce fear and distress in thousands of patients.

9

H.J. Eysenck and behaviour therapy at the Maudsley hospital

H.J. Eysenck is a prolific writer of immense scholarship who has a penchant for espousing some extremely dubious causes. Although there are about a thousand British academic psychologists, his publications alone account for an amazing one-tenth of all the citations they receive in learned journals. No doubt many of these arise from attempted rebuttals of Eysenck's unorthodox views on such subjects as the medical harmlessness of cigarette smoking, the dependence of one's vocation on one's astrological birth sign, and the reliability of statistical data and associated theories produced by the now notorious Sir Cyril Burt (whom Eysenck defended almost, but not quite, to the last). But many other citations must refer to his much more soundly based, if still iconoclastic, work on the practical and theoretical deficiencies of Freudian psychotherapy, and the virtues of 'modern methods of treatment derived from learning theory' (the sub-title of his influential book of readings *Behaviour Therapy and the Neuroses*, 1960).

Eysenck has made numerous empirical investigations and theoretical contributions of his own, but is equally important as the director until recently of the psychological laboratories of London University's Institute of Psychiatry, associated with the Maudsley and Bethlem Royal Hospitals, and as the founding editor of the journal *Behaviour Research and Therapy*. A large proportion of British work on behaviour therapy has emanated from this source, and many prominent academics and clinicians, now on both sides of the Atlantic, were under the Maudsley aegis at one time or another (for instance, S. Rachman, at first a prominent student of Wolpe's from South Africa, V. Meyer, C.M. Francks, H.R. Beech, I.M. Marks, R.J. Hodgson and many others).

Eysenck dedicated *Behaviour Therapy and the Neuroses* to the memory of J.B. Watson, and more than anyone else has founded his ideas on Pavlovian methods and theories. But it is worth noting that some of the credit for both the iconoclasm and the self-consciously scientific tone which characterize Eysenck's Maudsley school of thought should go to Henry Maudsley himself, who came to London from Ribblesdale via Cheadle in the 1860s, and by 1913 had established sufficient influence as a consultant psychiatrist and author to persuade the London County Council (with the help of a bequest of £30,000) to build the hospital, with the stipulation that it should always have close associations with London University. Maudsley was a proudly sceptical positivist who violently attacked introspection, emphasizing the limitation of consciousness; vehemently asserted that psychology was essentially a matter of cerebral physiology; and claimed that the study of animal psychology would be essential to mental science (see Sir Aubrey Lewis's introduction to *The Pathology of Mind*, 1895/1979). In terms of the causes and cures of insanity his views were interesting and widely read, but are not always relevant here. However, he discussed 'hereditary disposition' as a causal factor (something H.J. Eysenck tends to stress, rather more narrowly than Maudsley did). He also believed that the 'action of circumstances' was important, and thus spoke of the need for taking patients' life histories and the need for adapting treatments to particular patients – these also are features of behaviour therapy as practised for instance by Wolpe in the examples given in the last chapter. The slightly behaviourist tinge to Maudsley's discussion of upbringing and early environment may be judged from the following quotations:

> In the mental organism we have really a plastic machinery which if taken in hand sufficiently early, may be manufactured to almost any desired pattern of feeling and belief. (1979, p. 541)

> Let anyone from his earliest years live in conditions in which he must, as a daily matter of course, without thinking of it, practise self-denial and self-control, subdue self-regarding impulses, feel, think and act for others, he will unless the original structure of his nature be hopelessly bad, be shaped into a good social unit and rule himself wisely. (1979, p. 542)

The 'being shaped' sounds Skinnerian; and how is the following for a precursor of Pavlov? – 'So much then concerning the origin and development of language; it is the highest display of reflex function' (1876, p. 504).

There is therefore a case that Maudsley behaviour therapy is in part a development of English Victorian belief in self-discipline and orderly habits, and not just a matter of importing Watson and Pavlov (and Eysenck) from abroad. (Interested readers should also consult *Principles of Mental Physiology with Their Application to the Training and Discipline of the Mind*, 1874/1896, by W.B. Carpenter, Registrar of the University of London, and of course Herbert Spencer's two-volume *Principles of Psychology*, 1855/1899.)

Nevertheless, nothing could be clearer than the fact that Eysenck himself, and most of his associates, see themselves as supplying 'the help which the application of learning theory in the hands of a competent psychologist may be able to bring' (1960, p. 20). Because of this, 'consistent, properly formulated theory', and 'experimental studies specifically designed to test basic theory' (Eysenck, 1960, p. 11), are given a high priority, along with the development of applications of the theory to applied problems. The method of counter-conditioning introduced by Wolpe has remained a source of inspiration, but has been developed in various ways, notably by *in vivo* or real-life acting-out of coping with a graded hierarchy of specific problems (e.g. Meyer, 1957). The most fundamental contribution of Eysenck himself to the solution of practical problems has perhaps been his support for the direct treatment of symptoms (shyness, sexual difficulties, phobias) rather than fanciful underlying causes. Of course this in itself is hardly new. Maudsley recommended late-night warm baths, or a good round of golf, to relieve insomnia, 'travel with a suitable companion' or a seaside holiday to lift depression, and the prevention of constipation by thrice-weekly enemas for practically everything. What makes Eysenck's emphasis on the treatment of symptoms valuable is its obvious quality as an antidote to the Freudian view of symptoms as mere surface indicators of far deeper problems and therefore, in themselves, of little importance.

But Eysenck has often been more concerned with strengthening the theoretical foundations of behaviour therapy than with the development of new applications, and the continuing theoretical self-criticism of the Maudsley group, as well as the objective evaluation of the successes and failures of their practical methods, is worthy of attention. The treatment of psychological disorders by the methods of behaviour therapy is discussed in other chapters; I propose to discuss here the learning-theory analysis of the *causes* of neuroses rather than their cures.

In a paper written not too long ago, Eysenck (1976) presents a lucid and succinct summary of the vicissitudes of conditioning theories of neurosis and summarizes some new approaches. A central problem for the learning-theory analysis of neurosis is that principles of learning are always assumed to produce adaptive and useful behaviour, but the essence of neurosis is that it is, superficially at least, unwanted and maladaptive. Neurotic problems are at the same time self-perpetuating and self-defeating – this is what Mowrer called 'the neurotic paradox'. The Freudian or psychoanalytic resolution of this paradox is to assume that there are unseen and disguised purposes being served by neurotic symptoms – these constitute a cry for help, or a defence against unresolvable personal conflicts, or an escape from inner threats more desperate to the individual than problems presented by the symptoms themselves. Watson attempted to sidestep the more imponderable aspects of Freudian theory by appealing to the classical conditioning of emotions produced initially by real-life traumas. The burned child fears the flame, a child who burns his hand on a black stove may come to fear neurotically all things black, and Little Albert, conditioned to fear a white rat, might in later life still feel uneasy about white fur coats.

But Watson's theory ignores the neurotic paradox even at the nuts and bolts level. Why should a child continue to fear flames if he is only burned once, and then sees flames for years without being burned? Most textbooks say that if the conditioned stimulus is presented often enough without its unconditioned motivator, the conditioned effects will dissipate and 'extinction' will take place. This is one part of the paradox – classical conditioning should be adaptive in the sense that conditioned effects should correspond to real experiences, but almost by definition neurotic fears are unrealistic. There are always some cases where having been bitten once by a dog seems to produce fear of all dogs, no matter that dozens of utterly friendly dogs are thereafter encountered, and it is the absence of the dissipation of fear in these cases that is one of Eysenck's concerns.

Conditioning by worrying

Eysenck's solution to the neurotic paradox to some extent follows Mowrer's, and could be said in one sense to have been anticipated by F.D. Roosevelt (1933) – the neurotic has nothing to fear except fear itself. Eysenck does not put it quite like this, of course; he refers instead to the 'incubation' or 'enhancement' of conditioned responses. This occurs when certain kinds of conditioned stimuli are presented by themselves, without other external sources of arousal or distress, after having first been paired with such an external source, perhaps in a single trauma, but possibly in a series of less notable associations. The theoretical distinction is that only some conditioned stimuli acquire 'drive properties'. This is not very well worked out, although the single clearest theoretical advance in conditioning theory over the past decade is the realization that some conditioned stimuli are different from others. There are two aspects to this. The first one, emphasized by Seligman (1970), in his 'preparedness' hypothesis, is that for any species, there are both natural and unnatural kinds of association between stimuli. The second aspect, which we may call the Franklin Roosevelt effect, is that almost any stimulus, or idea, but especially naturally unpleasant or exciting ones, may acquire their own, self-generating motivational effects. This is a radical departure in learning theory, since it means that internal and possibly subjective processes become relatively independent of the external environment, but it is a departure that in fact makes conditioning theories of neurosis considerably more realistic.

There is supporting evidence for this point of view in various animal experiments, in which cats (Wolpe, 1958) or dogs (Solomon *et al.*, 1953; Seligman *et al.*, 1968) receive strong electric shocks in a certain location. When they are put in the same place subsequently, they remain extremely afraid of it even though they receive no more shocks. In some cases they become more and more afraid each time they are returned to it, even though they receive no externally induced unpleasant experience whatever while they are there. You will see that I have stressed that it is *external* unpleasantness that is absent in these cases – the most straightforward explanation of the persistence or enhancement of anxiety is that it is the *internal* fear or arousal, which the animals experience as a consequence of the initial conditioning, that becomes strong enough to serve as an additional conditioning experience each time. Being afraid of shock, if you are afraid enough, may be almost as unpleasant as the shock itself.

Even Eysenck, who has an old-fashioned respect for animal data, notes that physical pain produced by electric shock is not necessarily identical to the unpleasant experiences believed to be involved in human neurosis, and that the theory needs expanding to incorporate various forms of frustration, conflict, disappointment and guilt, along the lines pioneered by Mowrer. There is also little animal data on the question of attractive as opposed to aversive drives, which may be strong enough sometimes to get locked into the same kind of positive feedback effect. Nevertheless, the experiments at the Maudsley by Rachman on human volunteers suggest that it is not entirely implausible to suggest that the intense sexual appeal to some people of inanimate objects such as rubber mackintoshes, handbags or items of female underwear may be partly due to this effect (the fetishist has nothing to be excited about except sexual excitement itself). However, as Gray (1982) (another of Eysenck's students) has suggested, many aspects of anxiety are basically physiological. Hence the same reactions of the autonomic nervous system, with the same ameliorating effects of appropriate sedatives and tranquillizers such as barbiturates and benzodiazepenes, may indeed be observed in many varieties of human distress as well as in animals' reaction to fearful stimulation.

Anxious thoughts, anxious words, anxious deeds and anxious feelings

This brings us on to the question of the relations between the purely physiological symptoms that may be associated with anxiety, the subjective mental states of threat and dread that may or may not accompany them, and the effects that either or both of these may have on what we actually do or say. Clearly we are now a long way from simple analyses of conditioning, but a serious and significant attempt has been made by behaviour therapists to come to grips with this theoretically difficult but practically important set of problems in the 'three-systems model', due originally to Lang and taken up by Rachman (1978; for a comprehensive review see Hugdahl, 1981).

Lang's constructive criticism of previous conditioning theories of fear and anxiety is that they consider anxiety to be a single 'lump' of an emotion, whereas there is a great deal of evidence to suggest that at least three measurable aspects of anxiety can vary quite independently. His alternative is to divide anxiety, as Caesar divided Gaul, into three parts, which can be dealt with separately by the therapist. The three systems are behavioural, 'cognitive/verbal' and physiological, or action, awareness and autonomic nervous system reactions. A possible criticism of this is that the cognitive/verbal system is still treated as a 'lump' whereas it too ought to be divided into various kinds of relatively rational self-labelling, attribution and verbal formulations of a person's problems, together with a variety of subjective feelings of panic and distress and awarenesses by the individual of his or her own actions and bodily symptoms. However, for practical and applied purposes, the three-way division works well, since separate measurements can be made of a patient's activities (either directly or by report), verbal feelings (by interviews, self-report, and systematic questionnaires, sometimes referred to as 'fear thermometers') and autonomic reactivity (by various physiological techniques, including electrical recordings for heart rate and sweatiness).

At the extremes, three kinds of patient can be identified.

1 The purely *physiological responder*: this patient does not think or say that he or she is anxious, and reports no problems of living such as being afraid to fly in aeroplanes, feeling nervous about

going into work, interacting with family members, or such like. In that sense the patient is not necessarily a psychiatric patient at all, but is frequently encountered by GPs as a patient complaining of faintness, dizzy spells, bowel problems or insomnia, or any number of other symptoms, identified by the person as merely physical and not psychological, but classifiable by others as having psychological causes. Almost everyone probably qualifies here at some time or another – one can have a pounding heart, or butterflies in the stomach, without necessarily feeling or being neurotic, but it is not a negligible problem, since vast quantities of various sorts of tranquillizing drugs are dispensed to deal with physical symptoms, and chronic cardiovascular problems such as high blood pressure or chronic digestive disorders may result from unidentified anxiousness of this kind.

2 The mainly *behavioural responder*: there may not be many people like this, but it is theoretically possible, at least, for avoiding behaviours to become fixed with little evidence of arousal in physiological systems and relatively little self-knowledge. It is also possible in theory that the behavioural responder is such as a result of neurotic (or real) fears which are simply avoided. A person might sincerely believe that they are not afraid of flying; they merely strongly prefer trains, and if enough trains are available any problem they have with aeroplanes is solved. Many people have quite irrational aversions to certain foods or to certain species of animal, but as long as they can eat other things and stay out of the way of cats (or pigeons, or spiders), then they may not show any sign of a tendency towards cold sweats or numbness of the limbs, and may describe themselves in an answer to a questionnaire or in conversation as fear-free. Arguably, the other components of anxiety here are merely disguised. In a serious case someone might claim to be perfectly relaxed and happy, while never leaving their house. This is agoraphobia – fear of open places or crowds – which is not uncommon and has been treated in various ways by behaviour therapists. It may be only when a new factor intrudes – a spouse dies, or children leave home, and going out to work becomes essential – that the necessity of confronting feared circumstances leads to panic attacks and the seeking of help.

3 The exclusively *verbal/cognitive responder:* the extreme case of this might be termed the Woody Allen syndrome, where someone is able to lead an entirely agreeable and productive life but wishes

to spend vast sums of money in order to talk for hours to a therapist about how neurotic they are. This extreme may be fictitious, but Lang first proposed the three-systems model after finding that subjects who had become accustomed by desensitization procedures to handle snakes, still described themselves as very afraid of snakes. Of course, we all have to do things that we don't like, or even are afraid of doing, and it doesn't mean because we do things, that we like doing them. But in many cases people's beliefs about themselves constitute their problem, and the verbally expressed beliefs are an appropriate target for modification. 'I'm shy', 'I'm unattractive', 'I'm hopeless at figures', 'I know I'll fail the exam', 'I'm sexually incompetent', 'I panic whenever I see a spider', 'I'm always anxious', 'I'm hopelessly neurotic': if held strongly enough, all these beliefs can be damaging, and of course in practical terms it is not the exclusively cognitive responders who are at risk (those students who say every year 'I know I'll fail, I know I'll fail', and then breeze in on the day and get Firsts). Rather, those people are at risk in whom the cognitive component is by no means independent of the other two but is actively perpetuating, or even initiating, unpleasant worry-induced insomnia and physiological over-arousal, and neurotic avoiding activities (Mahoney, 1974).

Variations in the causation of neurosis

It is reasonable to suppose that each of the three systems might have some special effect in the causation of neurosis, even though they are unlikely ever to be completely independent. Rachman (1977, 1981) uses the three-systems model to support his very sensible suggestion that there is more than one way of acquiring a neurosis, and that traumatic conditioning experiences are neither necessary nor sufficient as a cause.

Clearly, autonomic reactions can be sufficiently unpleasant in themselves to be bound up in neurosis, whether or not they started from external precipitating factors. Many people with phobic or even more general anxieties can report life events which they believe have an obvious relation to their fears. If a salesman has the misfortune to knock over and kill his own son when driving home, as a consequence of his car's brake failure, the trauma itself would surely be sufficient to produce feelings of guilt and anxiety associated with driving for some time afterwards. Anyone who has been in a car accident, or had their flat burgled, or been brutally raped, is likely to suffer after-effects connected to reminders of the horrible event. But not everyone who endures such nightmarish experiences suffers the same sort of after-effects and this is one reason for being sceptical about the pure conditioning theory. Rachman is particularly interested in the fact that air raids during the Second World War failed to produce widespread outbreaks of neurosis. There was no increase in the number of patients attending psychiatric clinics following air raids in this country. In Liverpool, Sir Aubrey Lewis noted that although eighteen volunteers were trained as auxiliary mental-health workers to comfort those made anxious both during and after raids, there was, it turned out, no comforting necessary. This is probably something of a special case, since a shared threat from a known enemy has some very peculiar consequences for both individual and group emotions (not all of them desirable, I think, as the Falklands episode shows). But it directed Rachman's attention to social factors in neurosis, and rather belatedly behaviour therapists are adding these factors into their theories.

That the disasters of war are not without their after-effects is amply demonstrated by the studies of shell shock in the First World War and of combat fatigue in air crew in the Second World War. People in Northern Ireland are not untouched by the troubles, and children especially show symptoms of anxiety related to physical threats and social tensions (children, but only a few, also developed anxiety symptoms attributable to air raids in the Second World War). Nevertheless, Rachman is right to point out that the incidence of neurosis cannot be predicted from the incidence of externally produced traumas, and this is incompatible with a crude Watsonian conditioning theory.

Equally, vast numbers of people are afraid of snakes and spiders, even though they have had no obviously traumatic experience associated with these creatures, and many patients with crippling neurosis can report no precipitating event. The line now taken by Rachman (1977, 1978) and Eysenck (1976) is strongly influenced by Seligman's rather vague idea of preparedness. Children are commonly afraid of the dark, but not of their pyjamas, and commonly afraid of live animals, especially slimy or wriggly ones, but not afraid of electric plugs, sharp knives and scissors, or bottles of pills, which are in fact much more dangerous and have often been deliberately associated with active parental disapproval (this may be over-rated as an aversive stimulus for the human young). Sociobiologists might claim therefore that we have an inherited tendency to fear the dark and to fear snake-like and spider-like animals, perhaps in common with other primates, although for obvious reasons we have no genetically determined propensity to become afraid of scissors or plastic bottles of pills. Behaviour therapists are not usually so explicit, but a vaguer version of preparedness almost certainly contains at least a grain of truth, and is extremely convenient for explaining variability in conditioning effects. For instance, there are two reports of attempts to replicate Watson's experiment with Little Albert (see pp. 86–8), both of which failed. Eysenck (1976) is able to point to the fact that in these attempts iron bars were banged while infants were confronted with inanimate objects such as curtains or a wooden duck. These stimuli would not have the preparedness value of a live rat, which would be sufficient to account for the failure of the infants to become afraid of curtains or of wooden animals. Simply in attention-getting value alone, a live animal which moves, wriggles its nose and occasionally stares one in the eyes is certainly likely to be a more effective item in any sort of learning or information-gathering process than the fact that curtains happen to be present. Within learning theory, this can all be encompassed by appealing to selective attention.

Vicarious learning and the social transmission of information

Rachman (1977) wishes to augment the idea of conditioning by experienced external events with learning via 'vicarious and informational transmission of fears'. This seems extremely sensible, although there is relatively little experimental evidence that can be quoted in support of it. In relation to the three-systems idea, Rachman speculates that external conditioning will act most directly on behaviour and on physiological response, while in fears learned by imitation or 'informationally' (e.g. by a child watching unsuitably violent films on television) the subjective/verbal system will predominate. Since he quotes no evidence at all in favour of this speculation we should not feel bound by it. The important thing is that children especially, as Mary Cover Jones suggested, but possibly adults just as much, and adolescents even more so, are sensitive to knowledge derived from their peers, and this is only one source of cognitively based information. If anything, children have a tendency to seek out excitingly gruesome stories of monsters, and ghosts, and bogeymen, but excessive exposure to such things might conceivably lay the seeds in young minds for later neuroses, to say nothing of causing nightmares immediately afterwards.

The boundary between the rational and the neurotic in responding to the numerous sources of more mundane knowledge that we have available to us as adults is often blurred. Is it neurotic to lose sleep over our own job if a colleague is sacked (or if we receive dire warnings in the post from the Association of University Teachers), or to worry about having breast cancer or genital herpes after repeatedly coming across magazine articles on these topics? Surely not. And how much insomnia, or distraction from normal daytime activities, is appropriately caused by contemplation of the horrors of nuclear war? It is certain that such questions are unanswerable in terms of Rachman's theories, but almost as certain that they are unanswerable in any terms. The virtue of Rachman's critical examination of conditioning theory is that it acknowledges overheard old wives' tales, second-hand traumas, social norms and the cultural transmission of information as possible modulators, or even as determinants, of individual emotional experience.

Conclusions

Eysenck's own learning-theory model of neurosis (1979) is considerably less liberated from the crude Watsonian assertion of conditioning than is Rachman's work, and differences of opinion concerning other developments, especially cognitive behaviour modification (Meichenbaum, 1977: see p. 153), abound. However, the emphasis on the special factors involved when anxiety-provoking ideas acquire their motivational force (see p. 114), and the willingness to consider inborn and natural patterns of fear as well as individual differences in personality, together with the separate treatment of subjective, physiological and behavioural factors in the three-systems model (see p. 116), all show that the Eysenckian school of thought is capable of change and development.

10

B.F. Skinner on language and life

Although B.F. Skinner has never been actively involved in any field of applied psychology, or seriously pursued any form of experimental research other than that involving rats and pigeons in Skinner boxes, he turned voluntarily in mid-career to the wider reaches of human psychology, making the change at about the same point as Watson's less premeditated switch to advertising. I should make it clear at the outset that in general I regard Skinner's (and Skinnerian) efforts in this direction as largely sterile, pointless and misguided, but these efforts are at least worthy of inspection; and it is arguable that in some limited areas, such as the management of otherwise intractable conditions like chronic schizophrenia, anorexia nervosa and very severe mental retardation, worthwhile contributions to important practical problems have been made. We may consider separately Skinner's discussion of human language, which is almost universally denounced, and is probably underrated; the extension of Skinnerian methodology to special clinical populations, which has been relatively widespread but is undoubtedly overrated by its advocates; and

Skinner's larger recommendations for the organization of entire human societies or communities, which have received a surprisingly large amount of attention, although hardly anyone agrees with them.

Language as a form of learning

Skinner's book *Verbal Behavior* (1957) is very long, and extremely boring to read, partly because of ugly and unnecessary neologisms like 'mands' (for demands and requests), 'tacts' (for otherwise naming and commenting in things) and 'autoclitics' and 'intraverbals' (which are supposed to cover just about everything else). The book, although dedicated to Skinner's young daughters as his 'primary sources', is not predominantly about the acquisition of their first language by children. Rather, it makes an ambitious attempt to explain every aspect of the adult use of language, including poetry and metaphor and problems of composition such as self-editing and style. Alexander Pope represents the conditioning effect of rhymed couplets on intraverbal repertoires, James Joyce's *Finnegans Wake* is the classic example of multiple thematic sources leading to the recombination of fragments in extended verbal frames, and W.S. Gilbert is amusing because polysyllabic rhymes allow multiple sources of strength to overflow normal limits. This may or may not be an acceptable form of literary analysis, but Skinner's critics are surely right when they suggest that James Joyce is rather a long way away from rats in Skinner boxes.

Two-year-olds, however, are not as far from rats as James Joyce is, and perhaps a 1-year-old child is more like a rat than like a literary critic (or like a professor of linguistics). There is thus at least an initial justification for looking at early language acquisition in terms of learning processes. But first Chomsky (1959), and then other linguists and psychologists (e.g. Lenneberg, 1967), came down on Skinner so heavily that for a time it seemed as though 'learning to talk' actually involved no learning from experience or interaction with a social world whatever, but was just a pre-programmed event that happened to all babies, rather like teething, but with innately determined syntactical structures bursting through (some sooner than others) instead of teeth.

In fact Chomsky (1976) still says that as far as he is concerned, learning to talk might just as well be instantaneous – any gradual changes that might look like learning by experience (and all differences between one child and another) are better ignored. That may be all very well for Chomsky, but few psychologists would want to turn their backs completely on the data that can be gathered by actually studying the progress of an infant's development. However, the strength of Chomsky's reputation as a linguist, and the fact that many of the arrows aimed by him and others at Skinner's book undoubtedly found good marks, has meant that Skinner's theory in particular, and learning theories of language acquisition in general, have received even more ignominy than is their due.

I have lost count of the times students have told me that Skinner is wrong because 'by his method it would take a million years to learn a language'; 'children do not just copy their parents, they make up new words (sentences) they have never heard before, and say things like "mouses" which they have never been reinforced for'; 'according to Skinner children always pick up language from their parents, but isolated children can invent their own'; 'it is ridiculous to say that we have to talk faster or speak louder if we want something badly'; 'according to Skinner rats could be trained to talk if they lived long enough'; 'how could we talk without learning grammar'; 'speech involves re-combining the same elements in different orders, and you can't explain saying things in order by learning'.

These are all interesting ideas, but they bear very little relation to what Skinner himself actually said (and of course it might just be possible that someone could improve on Skinner without necessarily having to become Chomsky). To start with the minor points: first, Skinner does not say we could teach rats to talk; in fact he goes to the opposite extreme of saying that we could not train a cat to miaow to be let out or to get food, because animal vocalizations are only fixed emotional responses (1957, p. 464). In fact cats can be trained to miaow for food (Molliver, 1963) in the laboratory, and all cats I know of miaow to get out. The form of most mammalian vocalizations is fixed, and so to a large extent is the form of human crying, laughing, screaming and groaning. But of course many birds can produce the phonetic part of speech, if nothing else. Skinner says that the initial babbling of human babies 'is undoubtedly an evolutionary product' (i.e. innate) and that perhaps the human female makes innate responses to the innate cries of her baby. He is thus not completely against innate influences on human language even though he can certainly be accused of not taking human innate abilities enough into account.

Secondly, he takes innate abilities enough into account to acknowledge that 'Occasionally . . . two or more children have grown up in partial isolation from established verbal communities and have developed fairly extensive idiosyncratic verbal systems' (1957, p. 462). Nothing much is made of this, but it is surely not unreasonable to emphasize that normally people's speech is very strongly determined by their verbal environment (e.g. regional dialects and class differences, to say nothing of differences between English and Basque, Bantu and a certain Brazilian Indian language which normally has the object in sentences first).

Thirdly, it is true Skinner says that those who find talking rewarding will be enthusiastic talkers, but he is not silly enough to have failed to notice that there is more to talking than volume: 'there is no relation between the energy of the behaviour and the magnitude of the effect achieved. We sometimes shout to get action, but a whisper will have the same effect under other circumstances' (1957, p. 204).

Fourthly, neither was Skinner so foolish as to suggest that children copy everything from their parents, or have to be separately reinforced for every single compound utterance they have the potential ability to make, thus requiring the various fictitious estimates of language acquisition in units of thousands of years. Most, though not all, children copy a great deal from their parents (and from teachers, little friends and the Incredible Hulk). Even Chomsky, in the course of his famously critical review, says 'it seems beyond question that children acquire a good deal of their verbal and nonverbal behavior by casual observation and imitation of adults and other children' (1959, p. 42). And, on the next page, 'As far as language acquisition is concerned, it seems clear that reinforcement, casual observation, and natural inquisitiveness (coupled with a strong tendency to imitate) are important factors, as is the remarkable capacity of the child to generalize, hypothesize, and "process information".' But Chomsky received no academic reinforcement for this sensible even-handedness, and so stopped it (1976, 1980).

But although any babies (for instance those born deaf) who

could not imitate speech would be at a crippling disadvantage in language acquisition, imitation is certainly not the whole story, as Skinner himself observed. One thing that seems to happen is that children learn 'units', or 'segments', or 'fragments' of speech which can then be 'composed' into new combinations. As Skinner puts it, '*He singed* is obviously *composed* from separate elements' (1957, p. 121). This is the same simple argument as that derived from 'mouses', 'Daddy typewritering' and all other cases where English-speaking infants charmingly use parts of speech in new but wrong ways (foreign children can do this as well, but not as often, since there are few languages where rules have to be broken as often as in English). Skinner goes to some lengths to try and explicate what is happening, but unfortunately seems to have had a phobia about the word 'rule'. In *the boy runs*, the final *s* is a unit which is related to current activity by one person; in *the boys run* the same unit (*s*) has other functions – denoting plurality; and in *the boy's gun* a very similar sound is now a unit which indicates 'possession' (1957, pp. 121, 331–67). Chomsky had no trouble in pointing out that this particular unit has inconsistent functions, and made the incontestable claim that what Skinner is doing does not seem very different from traditional grammar. But Skinner is quite ready to admit that in the case of *the boy runs* his description of the *s* 'can scarcely be said to be an improvement upon the traditional statement that *runs* is a "verb in the third person singular and the present tense"'. What Skinner ought really to have said is that infants have to *learn* rules about the meanings of individual speech elements, and in addition rules about how to put such elements together, and since this is on the face of it a matter of learning from experience, perhaps we can consider it as a special case of more general processes of learning, some of which may be observed even in rats.

What Skinner in fact wrote was that all these different functional units exist, and that they and the process of assembling units into phrases and sentences depend upon 'the environment' and 'the verbal community'. There is undoubtedly an awful lot missing from this, and it is probably hopelessly inadequate as a theory of language acquisition. On the other hand, even though it is limited it is nothing like as implausible as the 'straw man' version of Skinner's theory which tends to be put forward by his supporters as well as his opponents.

If there is any doubt about Skinner's commitment in *Verbal Behavior* to a doctrine of language as a system of re-combinable elements, consider his relatively original speculations about the meaningful units usually called 'morphemes' (1957, pp. 121–3). Conventionally it would be assumed that *dest* in *destroy* and *destructible* means the same thing (has 'functional unity', according to Skinner) even though it is never used by itself. Skinner believes the same thing is probably true of even smaller elements. The *sp* in *spit*, *speak* and *spew*, he thinks, has to do with things coming out of the mouth, which is related to dispersal or radiation from a point in *sputter*, *sprinkle*, *spray* and *spoke*, *spire* and *spur*. And an *-each* ending is associated with noises in *screech*, *preach* and *teach* – hence, *speech*. The probability that children pick up or invent their own units of this kind is attested to by the fact that one of Skinner's daughters, when 6, thought, reasonably enough, that *-nese* in Chinese and Japanese described something about the shape of eyes.

The big problem for Skinner (or, if you like, one of his big problems) is that he vacillates between leaving everything outside in the environment – as he would like to – and putting things inside the head of the learner – as he finds he has to. A simple example of the latter occurs in his discussion of metaphor. He notes that many dead metaphorical expressions such as 'dull as ditchwater' or 'red tape' are not creatively metaphorical because we use them automatically in accordance with convention, without having ever seen dull ditchwater or actual bureaucratic red tape tying up bundles of paperwork. However, his daughter, on tasting fizzy soda water for the first time, remarked that it tasted 'like my foot's asleep' (1957, p. 92). This 'raises several difficult problems in the analysis of behaviour', because the tingling pins-and-needles sensation in the foot is not part of the outside environment which Skinner can observe, but inside his child's head and out of his behaviourist reach. Skinner's solution is to call it 'a private stimulus' and eventually (1957, pp. 130–46) private stimuli have to play a large part in generating ordinary 'verbal behavior'. This leaves Skinner wide open to Chomsky's charge, at the end of the egregious book review, that he is a closet mentalist. But if the rest of us are willing to come out and admit that speech is always controlled by internal mental structures of some kind, then there is no great difficulty in attributing some aspects of these mental structures to processes of learning.

That in itself would not take us very far of course. It does not say much about what Skinner calls, in his own quotation marks, 'putting in the grammar' (1957, p. 337). Perhaps we should leave all this to the linguists, and I have no business discussing psycholinguistics here. But it is only fair that Skinner should get some credit for wrestling with the issues, even though he ended up tied in knots. He may not be the only one locked in a permanent half-Nelson by the fact that knowledge of the word (semantics) always seems to be wrapped around behind one's neck when one tries to face up to 'Order, design and "deliberate" composition' (1957, p. 312). Skinner admits that it is usually crucial that the speaker has to 'know what he is saying', and that what is permanently or transiently 'known' is a separate part of the system which has control over the other sort of system which we describe as experiences of 'knowing'. This he relates to 'The notion of an inner self', although of course his own way of trying to duck out of the painful bind this causes the radical behaviourist is to insist that all these things ought to be labelled in terms of responses, behaviours and private stimuli. For example, 'There are *at least two* systems of responses, one based upon the other. The upper level can only be understood in terms of its relations to the lower' (1957, p. 313, my italics). But the 'systems of responses' he is talking about here are all inside the head and are completely equivalent, in their explanatory role, to what other people would call semantic knowledge and grammatical rules, and in this sense are not a million miles away from what Chomsky used to refer to as 'deep structure' and 'surface structure'. I wouldn't want to have to say in either case exactly what the up/down dimension refers to, but the important point is surely that knowing what we are trying to say is somehow different from the techniques we use in actually saying it. Or, the processes of decoding what hits the ear or eye in listening or reading are separate skills or abilities, and different from understanding meaning.

The independent and sometimes arbitrary nature of 'available grammatical practices' Skinner illustrates by claiming that the same headline message would be communicated in English newspapers by 'Death of the King', and in American ones by 'King Dies'. 'Student Grants Halved', 'Government Halves Grants' and 'Grants: Government Halves' would all give rise to the same sinking feeling.

So, Skinner's attempt to apply his approach to psychological questions to the contentious matter of human language is generally regarded as a failure, but in dealing with some of the complexities involved in this, he is not so green as he is cabbage-looking. His insistence on sticking to the formulae of private stimuli, and internal response systems, which all have to be discussed as if they were part of the outside environment or just another kind of overt behaviour, now seems ridiculous. It probably means he missed several crucial points, but it doesn't mean he missed *all* the crucial points. He was perfectly aware that his children said new and strange things which they had never heard before, and that we have to explain how phrases, sentences (and books) are composed and created. If a single testable hypothesis can be inferred from all that he wrote, it is that all aspects of language use are gradually learned and are primarily a function of the experience of the individual in a society that uses language. It is ironic that although Chomsky, or the subject matter, beat Skinner in the theoretical wrestling match by several falls to nil, much current research in psycholinguistics ignores Chomsky's advice that the important things are all innate and language acquisition might just as well be instantaneous. It concentrates instead on examining the very complex interactions in a baby's life which seem indeed to be variables that affect the child's acquisition of language (for instance, the details of the interactions between mothers and babies: see Coltheart and Harris, 1983; Harris *et al.*, 1983).

It is sometimes pointed out that it is even more ironic that research which shows the importance of the attention and wishes of the child, and the gestures and eye movements of the mother, takes us back to the learning-theory account of language acquisition given in St Augustine's *Confessions*, which has considerable priority over Skinner's in descriptive detail as well as publication date (*c.* AD 400). Roughly translated, this reads:

> I have since observed how it was that I initially learned to speak. It was not that I was actively taught words by any set method (as I was other things afterwards). But I myself tried to express my thoughts in order to get what I wanted and did this first by broken cries and various motions of my limbs. These did not express all that I willed or to whom I willed it, and by a specially evolved innate process I started to practise various sounds and

remember them. When my elders named something, and turned towards it when they spoke, I was able to see and remember that they made a certain utterance in connection with the object they were interested in. This was made plain by their bodily movements, which are, as it were, a universal natural language, in the form of expressions of the face, glances of the eyes, gestures of the limbs, and tone of voice, which all indicate expectancies of seeking and finding or avoiding and rejecting. And thus, by constantly hearing vocal elements, as they occurred in a variety of sentences, I gradually learned what the word-elements and their order stood for, and when I had practised making these sounds with my own mouth I was able to give utterance to my own ideas and wishes. (Augustine, 1929, p. 8).

This does not leave very much for Skinner to take the credit for, but there may even now be some mileage left in the notion that the motives and goals of the infant in listening and speaking are important in the context of the gradual learning of a particular first language. Such language starts with innate babbling and continues initially through the medium of social interactions, in which tone of voice, facial expression and other non-verbal activities are important props.

Skinner's recommendations for cultural engineering

Although some flotsam and jetsam may be salvaged from the wreckage of his theory of language, and there is some demonstrable practical value in the application of behaviourist methodology in the mental health field and in special education, Skinner's application of his ideas to the problems of society at large are almost completely worthless. In one sense Skinner could claim to have squarely confronted the question of applying experimental psychological principles to real life, since he has attempted to define the best future course for human civilization. However, in the light of what he has actually come up with, it perhaps would have been better for the reputation of the subject if he confined his attentions to the animal laboratory.

To put it bluntly, Skinner seems to be against almost all human emotions, and aspirations, ideals and values, as these are normally construed. One doubts if this is because Skinner himself is an unemotional and unfeeling person, because a reading of the two volumes of autobiography he has recently chosen to present us with suggests an intensely ambitious man with personal emotions of Dostoevskian intensity. Before taking up psychology he led a bohemian life in Greenwich Village, New York, trying to be a novelist, and the descriptions of his behaviours given in his autobiography do not suggest remoteness or detachment. For instance, Skinner tells us that after the break-up of an affair with a woman called Nedda, he used a red-hot wire to brand his own arm with the letter N, with such success that scars remained for decades afterwards.

In his utopian novel *Walden Two* (1948), and in essays on social philosophy such as *Beyond Freedom and Dignity* (1972), Skinner has discussed at length the problems of self-control and the necessity that we abolish 'autonomous man' by exercises in behavioural engineering. In his ideal world there would be no war, but neither would there be any emotions of personal triumph, or frustration, admiration of heroes, or envy or jealousy of others, or competitiveness or sorrow. It is in some ways reminiscent of Aldous Huxley's *Brave New World*, which made use of Watson's behaviourism, and Skinner seems to follow Watson not only in a contempt for democracy and free speech, but also in such details as 'The creative artist may manipulate a medium until something of interest turns up' (1972, p. 194; cf. Watson, 1931, p. xx).

In *Walden Two*, as in *Brave New World*, children are systematically conditioned in ways which the community regards as important, and for Skinner self-control is at a premium ('The evolution of a culture is a gigantic exercise in self-control': 1972, p. 215). This is done by giving 2- and 3-year-olds lollipops covered in sugar, with the instruction that if the lollipop is licked, it will be confiscated, but if they can keep it unlicked for the whole day, they will be allowed to eat it in the evening (1948, p. 107). Older children return from exhausting hikes expecting a hot supper, but are then made to stand in front of their bowl of soup for five minutes without eating it. Later, the same thing is done with all jokes or talking or fidgeting forbidden, and after five minutes half the children, randomly chosen, are allowed to eat their soup so that the other half can stand stoically by, supposedly having envy and resentment stunted. Tolerance to other annoyances is built up 'by having the children "take" a more and more painful shock' and getting used to enjoying drinking their cocoa without any sugar (1948, p. 108). In some ways, it is remarked, English public schools used to have quite good behavioural technologies. However, in Skinner's utopian communities no team games are allowed, and no one is supposed to compete with anyone else. He makes idiosyncratic exceptions in the cases of tennis and chess, but here there are to be no tournaments. Serious pursuits such as playing string quartets and practising arts and crafts are, on the other hand, encouraged (occasional references are made to William Morris's *News from Nowhere*).

There is of course no unadulterated fun, which Skinner is puritanically against. As an undergraduate, I heard Skinner give a lecture in which he argued mainly against the evils of playing cards (which he did not consider a useful activity) and for making Dostoevsky incomprehensible to future generations. It has occurred to me once or twice since then that I, among other members of the audience, might have been better off spending more late nights studying, and fewer playing cards, but Skinner's contempt for the study of literature and history is inexcusable, especially as he himself is well read, particularly in the literature of Utopias. The library at Walden Two is deliberately restricted to the two or three thousand books which the Planners believe to be the most elevating or useful: 'We don't attach economic or honorific value to education . . . we don't need to teach "subjects" at all. . . . Our children aren't neglected but they're seldom, if ever, *taught* anything' (1948, pp. 119–20).

In the real world, as opposed to the ideal one, Skinner is not quite so much opposed to formal education. But, as many critics have pointed out, Skinner's ideal world is paternalistic and authoritarian from top to bottom – with the Skinner figure at the top, admittedly playing God. The serfs begin work at an early age, and because of their early conditioning they 'get escape from the petty emotions which eat the heart out of the unprepared' and 'are spared the emotions characteristic of frustration and failure'. As compensation, lacking these distractions, 'They get immeasurably increased efficiency' (1948, p. 112). Only the Planners (mostly psychologists) at the top and the Managers in the middle have to suffer the trials and tribulations of administrative decision-making. If the system works, everyone has happiness and peace of mind, in moderation.

Another of the benefits of Walden Two is 'the satisfaction of pleasant and profitable social relationships' (1948, p. 112) but, as in other closed communities, these seem rather peculiar to outsiders. No one is ever allowed to say thank-you; it is customary to terminate conversations very abruptly if one becomes even slightly bored; and discussion of the Code, which stipulates these practices, is forbidden. The Code includes the Ten Commandments, and an unspecified number of other rules, which the Planners may change from time to time. 'The rules are frequently brought to the attention of the members' (p. 164). Some rules are posted (e.g. over the bathtubs), little pamphlets on jealousy and gluttony are distributed to 10-year-olds, and there are compulsory Sunday meetings with a sermon designed to maintain observance of the Code. Although this is borrowed from organized religion, and music is played to inspire group loyalty, and poetry is read to supply a common stock of literary allusions, religious belief as such is said simply to dwindle away, along with smoking and drinking, as a consequence of the earthly satisfactions of life in Walden Two.

One of the few aspects of social life which rings some sort of a bell today concerns the role of women. Skinner might receive high marks from some feminists, since the equality of women is rigorously enforced, even to the extent that they occupy equally with men the highest positions Skinner has to offer, as Planners. The role of women as wives and mothers is referred to as 'a tradition of slavery' going back thousands of years. This tradition is broken in Walden Two, since there are no homes or families in the normal sense. The children are all cared for by experts (of both sexes) instead of their mothers, and all prejudices regarding the proper occupations of the sexes are broken down. There is still marriage and child-bearing, with both taking place in the early teens to minimize the frustrations of adolescence. Couples require the permission of Managers to get married, and are supposed to accept refusal meekly if they are not well matched. It is anticipated that eventually the complete breakdown of the family unit will allow for selective breeding. With permission, marriages can be annulled and new ones contracted, but seductions and sexual jealousies are not allowed to disturb the tranquil and orderly ant hill. Although deeply puritanical, Skinner has no plans to dispense with sexuality, as he proposes to dispense with team sports and popular entertainment, and in fact in a recent lecture on the management of ageing he suggested that older intellectuals should give up chess in order to preserve their diminished cognitive energies, and devote the time saved to whipping up their flagging sexual appetites by the perusal of pornography (Skinner, 1983).

Walden Two seems to combine all the worst elements of the Amish communities in Pennslyvania, the state where Skinner grew up, the early kibbutzim in Israel, medieval monasteries and British boarding schools. Skinner quite unrealistically presumes that his version could be sustained without any punitive measures or ideological indoctrination. If any of his 15-year-olds are tempted by the bright lights of the big city, he supposes that he will only have to show them a filthy flat in a slum, and 'the home for indigents, the saloons, the jails', and they will come rushing back. As he simply wishes away all human weakness and ambition, and steps aside from conventional politics, sociology and economics, his proposals in Walden Two are completely unrealistic – but then so are all Utopias, and all attempts to establish isolated communes and experimental societies.

Is there anything to be gained from studying Skinner's proposals further? Perhaps we can dismiss at once what appear to be Skinner's purely personal preferences – he advances no argument in favour of tennis, chess and pornography, as against, for instance, snooker, bridge and cookery books. Although serious critics of Skinner's design often refer to it as 'enlightened despotism', part of the enlightenment seems to consist of a perverse distrust of some of the most harmless forms of human enjoyment of life, which owes more to the Pilgrim Fathers than to the psychological laboratory. Skinner doesn't like leisure, since it is not serious, and people are likely to distract themselves with trivialities such as cricket or fiction:

> In games and sports, contingencies are especially contrived to make trivial events highly important. People at leisure also become spectators, watching the serious behaviour of others, as in the Roman circus or a modern football game, or in the theatre or movies, or they listen to or read accounts of the serious

behaviour of other people, as in gossip or literature. Little of this behaviour contributes to personal survival or the survival of a culture. (1972, p. 179)

So we will have none of this at Walden Two. 'Life, liberty and the pursuit of happiness are basic rights. But . . . [t]hey have only a minor bearing on the survival of a culture' (1972, p. 180). Skinner really does mean, I think, in *Beyond Freedom and Dignity*, that we should do away with these basic rights as well. (In *Walden Two* the Skinner self-figure says that the Soviet experiment went wrong only because the Soviets dropped their attempts to abolish the family and religion, relied too much on propaganda and the worship of heroes, and still allowed the people in power to have the most wealth.)

But it would be a pity if, because of these truly appalling flaws in Skinner's application of his psychological ideas to the design of cultures, we turned away entirely from the whole issue. Political decisions are made all the time about vital issues such as the nature of payment for industrial work, education from cradle to grave, and individual conformity to social, legal and ethical norms. There is no reason why we should not sometimes think about these in psychological terms, and in this area Skinner's writings may at least stimulate opposing suggestions. There are also many smaller questions, especially to do with sections of the populations of mental hospitals, where piecemeal practical techniques on a small scale, which derive from some of Skinner's suggestions, may provide useful help. Some of these will be discussed in the next chapter.

11

Plain behaviour modification: rewards and withdrawal of rewards

In the learning theories of Skinner and Hull, the most fundamental operation is reward. In applying these theories to human psychology, both Skinner (1953) and Wolpe (1978) suppose that we can interpret many subjective experiences and cognitive habits, as well as obviously goal-seeking actions, in terms of histories of internal and private reward and punishment. In some cases this seems obviously right. Watching the World Snooker Championships is strangely satisfying, and even the sight of coloured balls dropping neatly into their pockets seems to elicit a special internal frisson. We remain glued to the set only because we like it (in spite of Skinner's free-floating disapproval of all spectator sports), and all the other things we do can in some sense be said to be rewarded – up to a point.

There are numerous objections to the all-embracing claims of these theories. We can at least entertain the fantasy of a peak moment of pleasure which is so breath-taking and overwhelming in intensity that it produces instant amnesia for itself and its build-up, and therefore has little effect on our future habits.

Although this seems a far cry from our day-to-day reinforcements of watching snooker and getting paid, the correlation between the emotional intensity of goal outcomes and subsequent knowledge is not always strong. Boring routines of practice may sometimes be more beneficial for both academic and musical skills than occasional celebrated successes, and also punishments can be better aids to memory than pleasures. And I can remember many things about academic meetings and conferences of such unrelieved tedium as to destroy all faith in the connection between subsequent retention of knowledge and emotional evaluation of any kind whatever.

Despite these and other quibbles, there is still a case that, in practical terms even if in no others, the manipulation of rewards remains a very powerful tool for the purpose of modifying overt behaviour. This carries most weight, again in practical terms, for the behaviour of those least likely to have alternative internal resources for the direction of their own behaviour, such as an objection to all rewards as a matter of political principle. In other words the manipulation of rewards has most effect on the behaviour of laboratory animals and children, and adults with the minds of children. Some regard all deliberate giving and withholding of tangible rewards as unethical, although civilized life as we know it would soon grind to a halt if everyone acted in this high-minded way. There are certainly many sensitive issues in the question of how to deal with persons who are severely handicapped in one way or another, especially if they are confined to institutions, and legal rulings as to the rights of patients have limited some behaviour-modification programmes, though more often in the United States than elsewhere (Stolz *et al.*, 1975). But the spectre of the behaviour modifier as invariably herding the mentally retarded into lavatories with a cattle-prodder and restricting access to films, fun and freedom, with the same goals as managers of the Gulag Archipelago, is unjustified as well as unjust. The horrendous problems of the individuals who may be treated by behaviour-modification methods are not of the making of the behaviour modifiers, many of whom are extremely dedicated and sensitive individuals, trying to surmount otherwise unsurmountable deficiencies in those in their care (Kiernan and Woodford, 1975, pp. 258, 295).

Behaviour modification with the severely retarded

Consider the problems to be faced in a school such as that discussed by Barton (1975). This is a school in a medium-sized subnormality hospital in a large northern city, attended by children for whom places cannot be found in other schools for the educationally severely subnormal (ESN(s) schools). In the 5 classes for the 70 children the mean intelligence quotients (IQs) ranged from 5 to 31 (where the average is 100), and 25 per cent of the children had mental ages measured in months for chonological ages measured in years. Some 38 per cent could not feed themselves, 61 per cent could not dress themselves, 52 per cent were not toilet-trained, 57 per cent had no speech and 36 per cent did not walk. The age range was 3–17 years. Physical difficulties such as seizures and sensory and motor impairment meant that any progress in such circumstances was likely to be slow, but behaviour-modification programmes designed for individual children suggested that it was not unobtainable. The general point is that if such children can be trained in basic self-help skills such as the following then their chances for the future, in terms of going to other schools and developing further social and manual skills, are immeasurably improved.

Toilet-training: six children of an average age of 13½ and with an average IQ of 10, who made up the next to the highest class, but were all incontinent, were given a toilet-training 'package' of the kind proposed by Azrin and Foxx (1971). This involved (1) taking them to a toilet every half-hour and giving them extra fluids, sweets, biscuits, praise and lots of attention when they successfully used it; but also (2) strapping them in a chair for half an hour, away from the class, if they had an accident (a 'time-out' procedure, used as a punishment). The results of this were slightly erratic, since two children were absent due to illness, but in the other four, accidents per week declined fairly dramatically.

Dressing: this was taught by a 'prompt and fade' technique. That is, the children were first both instructed and helped to dress themselves, but the amount of help given was gradually reduced. Social praise and congratulation were augmented with spoonfuls of sweet chocolate pudding as reward for the younger and more retarded participants. Large, loose elasticated garments were used to start with. This all seems perfectly sensible, and the method was strikingly successful even with children with an IQ of 8. Teachers thereafter saved time by not having to give as much help as before with coats, knickers and shoes, and the children were able to demonstrate the skills they had learned at school when getting up in the morning.

Movement and awareness of the environment: it is occasionally possible to elicit some response in individuals whose behaviour appears to be only vegetative. Fuller (1949) conditioned arm raising by injecting liquid food into the mouth of an 18-year-old who had barely ever before made any controlled movements. Barton (1975) reports that an 8-year-old girl with a developmental age of only 3 months seemed to learn very rapidly to make voiced sounds for the rewards given by 10-second activation of a large vibratory pad placed under her.

Language and social communication: the elicitation of basic movement and awareness is perhaps only worthwhile if it can be the starting point for much further development. At a different level of achievement, there have been many attempts to use the methods of behaviour modification to improve the skills needed for appropriate speech and social interaction. For, if this succeeds, it clearly provides the individuals concerned with access to other sources of information and help. It is sometimes said that language is given innately, and is acquired by all children independently of motivation and intelligence (Lenneberg, 1967; Chomsky, 1965, p. 58). For applied purposes, this is quite without foundation. There are very many particular kinds of language deficit and speech difficulty but also, in general, impairments of speech and comprehension necessarily go hand in hand with mental retardation. Barton (1975) quotes a single case of systematic improvement in the correct naming of pictures of 12 items that were originally misnamed by a profoundly retarded 15-year-old, when sweets were given for correct responses during tests.

Somewhat more subtle linguistic skills, as well as articulatory skills and object naming, are also susceptible to reward training. Stevens-Long and Rasmussen (1974) used food rewards and praise to persuade an autistic 8-year-old to use plurals correctly when he was describing pictures, and also to use longer and longer descriptions, in the form of compound sentences. Lutzker and Sherman (1974) used similar methods to promote subject–verb agreements for singulars and plurals when both retarded children and normal toddlers who had not yet started doing this described pictures. An important aspect of these forms of training is that (if necessary by training with large numbers of examples) the trainees generalize, or learn functional units, or learn rules so that, after being rewarded for saying 'boats are sailing' instead of 'boats is sailing', they can apply the rule to a new description, such as 'girls are riding', *without* having to be separately rewarded for each new instance of the rule (see pp. 127–8). Similarly, in linguistic analyses of remedial language training, it is taken for granted that 'practice and motivation' will serve the purpose of strengthening new linguistic structures (Crystal, 1979).

For normal children, waving goodbye is often a very early and popular form of social exchange, although greeting strangers by saying hello may sometimes be inhibited by shyness. In the retarded even these basics may require contrived and protracted training. Stokes *et al.* (1974), working with withdrawn boys in a home for the retarded, began gently pulling a boy's arm back and forth in the form of a wave when they met him, before giving crisps or sweets. Alternatively, sweets were waved about, followed by the boy's hand being waved, before they were delivered, as a 'visual prompt'. Following this, more realistic greeting responses, sustained only by the rewards of social interactions with reasonably enthusiastic training personnel, were observed.

Wanted and unwanted behaviours in the less severely retarded and in special cases

The basic methods of behaviour modification are the giving of both tangible and social rewards systematically for small steps towards all kinds of skills, and the equally systematic withdrawal of reward for antisocial or disruptive behaviours. The behaviour modifier may withdraw immediate social responsiveness to these misdemeanours by parents and teachers; or he may remove the learner from most possible sources of reward (often by isolating a child from companions and toys in a 'time-out' area) as a consequence of these unwanted acts. The methods have been found useful in a number of instances other than with very severely retarded children. Williams (1959) and Wolf *et al.* (1964) are often quoted for examples of very extended and intractable tantrums in young children of 2 and 3 years old (in these cases associated with hospitalization for other reasons), which disappeared when the tantrums resulted in the children being left in their rooms until the tantrums subsided. Both Wahler (1969) and Callias and Carr (1975) instructed parents of older children with more generally disruptive behaviours in similar deterrent techniques, with apparently satisfactory results. In the Callias and Carr report this was part of a more general programme in which clinical psychologists instructed the parents and teachers of retarded children in behaviour-modification techniques for accelerating the acquisition of various skills (the usual self-help necessities, and also helping in the house, communication, and miscellaneous matters such as training in wearing hearing aids) and for 'decelerating' many other things, including, hitting, hair-pulling, biting, throwing, smearing and tearing clothes, tantrums, screaming and head-banging. Both Wahler and Callias and Carr gave special training to parents with instructions via earphones and videotaped methods of feedback, where this was necessary.

The application of behaviour-modification methods in these instances may be judged as severe and unappealing, but they appear to be effective in dealing with problems to which no alternative solutions are available. There is similarly a case to be made for the application of controlled rewards in the symptomatic treatment of anorexia nervosa. In this syndrome patients (often but not always girls or young women) refuse to eat and may because of this die, if untreated. When hospitalized patients are allowed access to visitors and such privileges as listening to the radio and making telephone calls only if they gain a specified amount of weight (e.g. a pound in five days), weight gains ensue (e.g. Halmi *et al.*, 1975).

The use of tokens

A broom used in an experiment in 1965 has become, to some behaviour modifiers, an object of considerable veneration (e.g. Craighead *et al.*, 1981). Haughton and Ayllon (1965), working in a ward for chronic female schizophrenics, gave cigarettes to one of the patients only when she was holding the broom. As a result, the broom became a valued possession, and the patient stood holding it for long periods of time. The experimenters then asked two psychiatrists to make independent diagnoses of the broom-holding behaviour. One said that this behaviour was a stereotyped response of the kind commonly found in regressed schizophrenics, with the broom acting as a favourite toy, as might occur with a young child. The other, more imaginatively, proposed that the broom signified something more meaningful to the patient, and that to her it represented either her own child, or a phallus, or the sceptre of an omnipotent queen, or perhaps some combination of these. Behaviour modifiers believe that to the patient the broom represented cigarettes, and thus to them the broom represents both the fallibility of psychiatrists and the infinite malleability of all behaviour when rewards are dispensed by behaviour modifiers.

In the belief that extended control over rewards would lead to extended control over behaviour, tokens such as coins and chits were established in place of individual cigarettes as rewards, to be used by schizophrenic patients in the hospital as money, exchangeable at appropriate times for consumables or privileges. Examples are: personal chair, 1 token per day; choice of bedspread, 1 token per day; 20-minute walk in the grounds, 2 tokens; attending an off-ward religious service, 10 tokens; having a private audience with the ward psychologist, 20 tokens; having a private audience with a social worker, 100 tokens; choosing a television programme, 3 tokens; toilet articles such as toothpaste, comb and lipstick, 1–10 tokens; clothes and accessories such as slippers, skirt and handbag, 12–400 tokens. In order to obtain tokens patients had to earn them, either by useful self-care activities, or by on-the-ward jobs. Examples are: make own bed and clean area, 1 token; brush own teeth once per day, 1 token; act as waitress (for 10 minutes), 2 tokens; washing-up (for 10 minutes) 6 tokens; write names of other patients brushing teeth (for 30 minutes), 3 tokens (Ayllon and Azrin, 1968).

For obvious reasons such a system is referred to as a 'token economy'. There is no doubt that when it is well run, changes in the behaviour of patients, even chronic schizophrenics, may be observed, interpretable in terms of economic pay-offs. These include the hoarding, lending at interest, and stealing of tokens – the first two discouraged in at least one instance by a policy of token inflation (at 25 per cent per month: Atthowe and Krasner, 1968). There is equally no doubt that under even the best-run systems the patients remain schizophrenic, and although occasional transitions to normal working, via half-way houses, have been reported, there is no evidence that token economies produce 'cures'. In the United States, the setting-up of token economies has been discouraged by a number of legal rulings which forbid such things as limitations of patients' rights to attend religious services or to have their own chairs. Thus, many of the items and privileges used as reinforcers in the original schemes have been declared to be the legal rights of all patients. Also, it is now required that the legal minimum wages (in dollars) be paid for many of the duties which they originally performed (e.g. *Wyatt* v. *Stickney*: Stolz *et al.*, 1975; Kazdin, 1977). In the United Kingdom, the setting-up of such systems has proved not often to be feasible within the National Health Service (Thorpe, 1975).

In view of the ethical and legal problems raised by token economies, their high administrative cost, and the very limited therapeutic gains demonstrated, they cannot be said to have proved their usefulness. However, it is claimed that similar schemes have had beneficial effects without contravening legal rulings, not only in mental hospitals but also in special schools and residential institutions for various kinds of delinquent (Kazdin, 1981; Craighead *et al.*, 1981). At their mildest, such schemes have the benefits and limitations of various point, mark or gold-star award systems which have a long history in educational contexts (Kazdin, 1977).

12

Behaviour therapy and cognitive behaviour modification

The terms 'behaviour modification' and 'behaviour therapy' can be used almost interchangeably, although by and large it is the techniques used to dispel anxiety by Wolpe and the Eysenckian school that are called therapy, and the methods used by Skinnerians to try and build up new behaviours in retarded children or psychotic patients which are called modification. There is a certain amount of controversy surrounding cognitive behaviour modification, as might be expected. Much of this boils down to simple name-calling, with one side saying 'We must wake up to reality and start to recognize that people have cognitions and beliefs', and the other side saying 'Oh, no, people have only private stimuli and unseen responses, as we have said all along'. But at bottom is the fundamental ambivalence of radical behaviourists faced with cognitive processes, and an important practical dispute about which methods of therapy work best.

The argument for including thoughts and cognitions as part of behaviour modification has been put forward at length by Mahoney (1974) and Meichenbaum (1977). The starting point is the obvious contradiction between the early formulations of behaviour therapy, which described all clinical problems as 'maladaptive behaviour' and all therapeutic measures as 'reconditioning behaviour'; and the fact that many, if not the majority, of clinical problems are best described as disorders of thought and feeling. Some of the complexities of this situation are taken into account in the three-systems model, discussed in chapter 9, but the contradiction remains.

There is still a very hard-nosed view, which pops up occasionally in some surprising quarters, that as we can never be entirely sure about the contents of someone else's mind, we would be better off ignoring it and sticking to observable movements only. This is related to the opinion that consciousness is just 'the smell above the factory', which doesn't actually do anything useful. There is also the argument that since all the most important things are unconscious anyway, we need not bother much with the conscious part directly. This applies to Freudian unconscious emotional conflicts, but also to the fact that people are said to perform very complicated motor and perceptual skills, such as those involved in driving or playing tennis, while not thinking about the details of the actions involved. In some practical cases, the lack of effect of conscious desires may be part of the problem – someone may want to give up smoking, or stop being shy, or stop being afraid of heights, but this does not seem to be enough. More generally, feelings, cognitions and actions often seem to be independent of one another.

Those who want to include cognitions in behaviour therapy say that although that may be theoretically very interesting and difficult, from a practical point of view it is foolish to ignore the commonsense idea that a person's conscious thoughts and beliefs are among the most important determinants of their actions and behaviours, both in mental illness and in health. It may be true that some people occasionally do complicated things while unconsciously sleepwalking; chess masters do some incredibly clever computations intuitively; and some of us go back to sleep after having made firm conscious decisions to get up. But in the normal course of life many important decisions are premeditated. People have been known to get married and have babies by mistake, and others may become compulsive shop-lifters or commit murder while deranged. But there are very few reports that anyone has sold their house and bought another one, or completed a degree course, during a fit of absentmindedness.

Apart from hard-nosed scepticism, there are two answers which non-cognitive behaviourists give to the claim that cognitions arc important. Thc first is: '*Of coursc* thoughts and cognitions are important, and we have said so all along, but would you please not fall back into the disgustingly mystical habit of calling thoughts thoughts, instead of calling them by their proper names of private stimuli and behaviours.' The person who can say this with most justification is Wolpe, since from the beginning he did indeed talk extensively to his patients about their beliefs, instructed them to try to think differently, and asked them to have fantasies about things which made them anxious (see chapter 8).

With slightly less justification, Skinnerians also say that 'self-instructional training,' along with other kinds of cognitive restructuring, is what they have always recommended, but that these forms of therapy will only be properly scientific if we happen to describe them in terms of 'the role of private events in controlling behaviour' (Lowe and Higson, 1981, p. 82). Skinnerians tend to be extremely slippery customers in these arguments, since if ever they are taxed with the importance of mental events, they claim that Skinner has already included them in his system. For instance, Blackman, in his presidential address to the British Psychological Society (1982), insisted, 'It is quite clear that behaviourists such as Skinner recognize the reality of our subjective states, and try openly to fit such states into their general schema.' But there is a catch, since this is done 'without attributing special status to mental events', so that they end up being private stimuli and responses instead of thoughts and cognitions (Blackman, 1982, p. 337).

There are at least two reasons why it is better to be on the side of cognitions than on the side of private behaviours. The first is just clarity. If it is very often assumed that the behaviourists in question are denying the reality of thoughts and cognitions, this is largely because they persist with their taboo of special words for them. The second is that mental events surely *are* special, for one reason or another. Having undergone several hundred million years of evolution in order to acquire brains which are capable of thought and, in the case of most of us, decades of expensive and arduous education to help us to think, it seems very strange to classify our thoughts along with the wrigglings of the amoebae, although we saw that that was just what Watson, if not his later disciples, intended to do (see pp. 10 and 24).

Therapeutic considerations

Let us now return to applied questions concerning techniques of therapy, which after all are more important than terminological wrangles. From now on we can assume that everyone agrees that patients can be dominated by obsessional thoughts, can be panic-stricken by imagined disasters, and misled by erroneous beliefs, provided that we make simultaneous translations available in the jargon of different academic sub-cultures. The argument is: should we not try to try to work directly on the patient's obsessions, imaginings and beliefs instead of relying on the battery of behaviour therapy techniques already provided by Wolpe and others? This sounds straightforward enough, but in fact the difference between techniques called 'behaviour therapy' (following Ledwidge, 1978) and those called 'cognitive behaviour modification' is not always obvious. By and large, behaviour therapy includes the methods, used by Wolpe and others, such as assertion training and opposing anxiety by relaxation in systematic desensitization, which in theory are aimed directly at the patient's symptoms. Cognitive behaviour modification, on the other hand, attempts to change the patient's mind.

It may do this by rational argument and advice, emotional confrontation and brow-beating or by specialized exercises in self-instruction, self-awareness and rational analysis of problems. A patient (grown-up) who only feels secure in the company of his teddy bear may be told: 'Don't you think it would help your marriage if you gave up your teddy?', 'Don't you realize most adults manage without teddy bears?' 'It is ridiculously childish to sleep with a teddy bear', 'Practise saying to yourself every night "I don't need my teddy, I'm grown-up and I don't need my teddy"'. In Wolpean desensitization, the same patient might over a series of interviews be helped to relax while progessively imagining: teddy is at the bottom of the bed; teddy is on the floor by the bed; teddy is just in the next room; teddy is sleeping downstairs; teddy has been given to Oxfam.

Both procedures clearly involve mental processes, so that is not an issue. But often (though not always) in Wolpean procedures patients do not have to actively analyse their own problems but can passively follow the directions of the therapist. In other procedures patients are required deliberately to restructure their own thoughts or to engage in certain forms of positive thinking or otherwise helpful mental routines. I must say that it does not seem to me a hard and fast distinction and that it is just a matter of a large variety of possible procedures, all of which involve some measure of direction, persuasion, comfort and amelioration of anxiety by calming experiences. However, Ledwidge (1978) has provided a very thorough analysis of procedures, which he separates into two categories, and there remains a division between cognitive and behavioural treatments based on different theoretical traditions.

Ledwidge's point is that attempts to 'modify the client's pattern of thought (faulty premises, assumptions, attitudes and the like)' just do not work as well as methods which concentrate more directly on actions and on anxiety conceived as a bodily response. He agrees that 'thoughts and feelings do play a critical role in human behaviour' and that 'changing thoughts and feelings is the aim of behaviour therapy', but says that ten years of clinical experiences, and his extensive review of other controlled comparisons, have convinced him that 'the best way to change thoughts and feelings is to change behaviour directly; changes in thoughts and feelings will then follow' (1978, p. 371). There is a case to be made that the definition of a neurosis is something that does *not* respond to kind advice, rational discussion and self-help. Other problems such as smoking, alcoholism, drug addiction and disorders of sexuality are again usually resistant to direct appeals to the hearts and minds of the sufferers, and that is why therapists of all kinds have to resort to the more drastic or less predictable tricks of their trades. But the proof of the pudding is in the eating. Some problems may be less severe than others, not all patients (or therapists) have need of the same methods, and there is abundant evidence, as Wolpe (1978, 1981) freely admits, that some patients have cognitive problems that respond to cognitive solutions. The more cognitive methods are therefore worthy of a little further examination.

Albert Ellis's rational emotive therapy

Albert Ellis is a New York psychiatrist who, like Wolpe, started off as a Freudian but became disillusioned by the lack of practical effects of Freudian analysis on his patients. He originally specialized in marriage-counselling and sexual problems, and providing direct instructions and basic information in these areas could, at least in the 1950s, sometimes have very quick and very beneficial effects. Ellis turned from Freud first to Pavlov, and in a discussion of the origin of his methods includes an account of Pavlovian conditioning, partly in terms of the expectations that might have been engendered in Pavlov's experimental dogs. But on the rational grounds that patients can be talked to with rather more result than dogs, Ellis developed a diffuse, but he believes effective, system of therapy. It is not easy to summarize, but Ellis says it is minimal as far as the personal relationship between therapist and patient goes, and maximal as regards the directive and teaching element in their verbal exchanges.

A fundamental tenet is that thinking and emotion are usually related, and especially so in psychological problems. The ancient Greek formula that 'Man is disturbed not by events but by the opinions he forms about them' can be taken as a slogan for cognitive therapies, and in Ellis's bad emotions are seen as a function of irrational ideas and cures take the form of modifiying these or substituting better ideas. In the simplest form of the therapy, patients are told in no uncertain terms to look on the bright side, stop worrying and pull themselves together, but this is a fairly protracted process (several hours a week for months, but not, as in psychoanalysis, several hours a week for years). Also, Ellis is eclectic in his techniques, bringing in desensitization by familiarization with disturbing circumstances or actions, and even a certain amount of Rogerian 'positive regard' and respect for the patient by the therapist.

The 'rationality' should not be taken too literally – it is sometimes a matter of changing not unreasonable but counterproductive opinions into just as irrational but helpful ones. It is not necessarily more rational to be an optimist than a pessimist, but being pessimistic is usually less helpful, and is something to be discouraged in depressed patients. Ellis (1962) gives eleven basic irrational ideas which tend to be emotionally self-defeating and are commonly associated with psychological problems. A main theme is an inability to come to terms with life's ups and downs, and there also seems to be a lack of toleration for ambiguity and error. The first irrational idea, for example, is the belief that one must be loved and accepted by absolutely everybody – therefore rejection or loss of love is made very disturbing. The second is the perfectionist desire to be excellent in all possible respects and never to make mistakes. The third is the belief that badness should always be punished, so that blame and anger are engendered for one's own and others' shortcomings. Many other ideas come up in case histories, including the belief that self-discipline is impossible to achieve, that emotions cannot be controlled, that this is especially so if bad emotions have been caused by an unfortunate childhood, and so on.

The general thrust of therapy, then, is to convince the patient that nobody is perfect, everybody makes mistakes, and it is not the end of the world if X happens – 'If I try hard enough things will get better, I can conquer my irrational fears', etc. It is an important part of the procedure that patients practise saying to themselves statements that emerge in optimistic discussions with the therapist, or that they are explicitly directed to practise, sometimes with the help of 'homework' in the form of checklists and questionnaires. The patients have to break habits of saying, for example, 'She might reject me and that would be awful', 'I'm no good, my parents think I'm worthless', 'This is never going to get any better and it's all because I'm stupid', and to form new mental and overt habits of saying, instead, 'She might accept me and that would be wonderful', 'It's only my parents' opinion and I know I'm OK', 'There is no such thing as a stupid human being only a fallible human being, I can get better and I'm going to build new cognitive maps'.

As far as origins go, this is clearly related to an American tradition of optimism, self-improvement and self-confidence-building, which goes back to salesmen standing in front of a mirror in the morning saying 'I'm going to sell, sell, sell today', and continues in pep talks and half-time inspiration by football coaches. There is much to be said for pep talks, and self-encouragement of all kinds, but Ledwidge (1978) is entitled to his doubts as to whether these measures are universally successful in cases of severe psychological disorder.

A condensed version of an exchange which Ellis (1962, p. 296) says brought about the cure of a chronic psychopath goes like this:

THERAPIST Isn't your thick skin really nourished by your corrosive hatred of others, and doesn't that hatred in the long run corrode you?

PSYCHOPATH Hmm. . . . You've certainly given me something to think about.

THERAPIST Well you give it some real hard thought then. [*Psychopath exits, restructuring his cognitions.*]

Another success story given by Ellis (1971) concerns a couple who had been married for thirteen years without ever having had intercourse since, after initial difficulties, 'We thought we'd wait till maybe a more convenient time to work it out.' The therapist very quickly jumps in to tell them that their behaviour is due to (1) fear of failure and (2) sexual puritanism. They readily agree, having had strict and sheltered upbringings. They become convinced that all their guilt is irrational, but when the therapist gives them sexual exercises of the Wolpe type (see pp. 104–5) it transpires that they also have the irrational belief that all sexual relations should be spontaneous, and should not be artificially contrived. Once this error had been expunged by further instruction, the exercises did the trick, sexual relations proceeded as if they had never been absent, and the patter of tiny feet was soon heard.

An understandably less successful case concerned a graduate student who had initially had the psychotic belief that a guardian angel would protect him if he jumped in front of large trucks. Acting on this belief he received a very severe concussion, which for one reason or another dispelled his belief in the angel but which left him with a severe phobia for noises (connected with the fear that he would experience another concussion), insomnia, and remorse about his own stupidity, with suicidal depressions (Ellis, 1971, p. 179). An immediate course of rational therapy helped, but all the (post-angel) symptoms returned a year later, and protracted further therapy with much homework was necessary.

There seems no reason to doubt the value of rational argument used to change attitudes which are obviously self-destructive, but at the same time amenable to reason or to persuasion. Beck (1976) has recommended similar therapeutic techniques, especially in depression. If these work, all well and good, but there are certainly limits to the number of cases of severe mental illness that are likely to respond to arguments along the lines of 'If you examine things rationally there's really nothing to be afraid of' and 'Cheer up, it's not your fault, there's nothing to be depressed about'.

Meichenbaum's self-instruction

I still occasionally find myself remembering the instructions 'Look right, look left, look right again, before you cross the road', which were drilled into me at school as an infant. It has often been observed that children between about 2 and 5 may self-instruct or self-describe their own behaviour (e.g. 'Now Dolly is going to bed'), and although this is by no means a universal and ever-present phenomenon, a number of Soviet theorists have argued persuasively that the development of inner speech is an important element in the child's progress towards adult thought (Vygotsky, 1934/1962; Luria, 1961; Sokolov, 1972). Meichenbaum has suggested that artificially augmenting internal and overt self-instruction may assist in improving the behaviour of children judged to be 'impulsive' or 'hyperactive' – of which there are apparently such large numbers in North America as to almost constitute the norm (Meichenbaum, 1977). Older children (up to 10) as well as younger ones may benefit from posters and cartoons which contain such slogans as 'Look and think before I answer' and 'What does the teacher want me to do?' (cartoons may later become unnecessary, but even the most mature university students may sometimes benefit from reciting similar homilies to themselves before answering examination questions). The usual thing with young children is for an adult to model (demonstrate) the required self-control in such things as copying pictures, saying, as they unspontaneously perform the task, 'OK, what is it I have to do? You want me to copy the picture with the different lines? I have to be slow and careful. OK, draw the line down, down, good; then to the right. Good, I'm doing fine so far.' There is some evidence that this slows the children down and improves their performance when they do a similar task themselves, and that this is because they imitate the tactic of talking to themselves out loud. There is no evidence, however, that such procedures by themselves are a panacea for all impulsiveness and hyperactivity.

As Skinner certainly recognized, the area of self-control is a large one, and the day-to-day and year-by-year influence of what goes on at home and at school cannot usually be counteracted by an hour or two of isolated verbal training. More thoroughgoing intervention, sometimes with explicit retraining of parental behaviours towards their offspring, may be needed for oppositional (difficult) and hyperactive children (Wahler, 1969, 1980).

There is also little evidence that self-instructional training has any very profound effect on the thought and speech of chronic schizophrenics, which is often weird, delusional and over-inclusive (rambling). Behavioural techniques of reward and persuasion (see pp. 142–3) have been used in attempts to change these particular symptoms, among others, and Meichenbaum (1977) observed that patients who had been instructed to 'Give healthy talk, be coherent and relevant' began to repeat this exhortation to themselves. Further examples are given by Meichenbaum (1977, p. 75) of schizophrenic patients being explicitly encouraged to repeat to themselves 'I must not talk sick talk', 'Don't talk crazy', 'Stay on the topic, stay on the topic' and 'Don't ramble on, don't ramble on'. The effect this expedient has on the long-term prognosis of the patients involved appears to be extremely limited, but the last two suggestions may again come in handy for students writing essays (and for lecturers giving lectures, I know). The anecdote which expresses the difficulties as far as schizophrenics are concerned is about a paranoid person who believed he was Napoleon. He was arduously persuaded by the giving of tokens and by advice as regards self-instruction to say that he was John Brown, born in Chicago in 1940, rather than N. Bonaparte, born in Corsica in 1769, but after this achievement he pocketed his tokens, put his hand inside his jacket and asked all in the corridor as he left not to pay any attention to the John Brown nonsense, as he was really Napoleon (Wincze *et al.*, 1972). Verbal expression is not always the same thing as belief, and words may often disguise thoughts in many less extreme cases.

Stress inoculation and imagery

Meichenbaum (1977) also suggests that forms of self-instruction can be used to prepare those who know they have difficulties such as reacting with excessive anger or anxiety to certain personal interactions (e.g. personal strains at work, or visits to parents or in-laws). These appear to be fairly elaborate, including advance preparations, on-the-spot self-warnings and self-debriefings afterwards, such as 'I can work out a plan for this, it won't be too bad', 'Stay calm, stay calm, keep control', 'There was no need to take it personally, I don't have to be upset by that', 'It will all be the same in a hundred years, it isn't the end of the world'. It is surely true that time-honoured maxims and proverbs, and more recent slogans and self-instructions, play a role in some people's lives, and may occasionally be helpful in therapy, especially for mild sorts of personal emotional control. But equally Wolpe (1978) is not only whistling to keep up his own courage when he claims that self-instructions and simple maxims are not very much use in severe cases of anxiety. As an old proverb has it, 'panic fear is beyond all arguments'. As Wolpe says, many strong neurotic fears are triggered by things that the patient already knows to be harmless, and telling oneself to keep calm and that there's nothing to worry about is unlikely to be very much help during a panic attack. If it was, there wouldn't be such a need for therapies.

Behavioural treatment of obsessions and compulsions

The incidence of incapacitating obsessional and/or compulsive disorders is not high – certainly less than 5 per cent of psychiatric patients are classified in this way, although obsessional symptoms (or possession of an 'obsessional personality') may be fairly common in those who see no reason to seek professional help. Considerable attention, however, has been given to these disorders by behaviour therapists. That fact is particularly interesting in the context of this discussion, since a frequent feature of obsessive-compulsive disorder and, indeed, according to earlier writers, *the* defining feature of the syndrome, is the presence of obtrusive thoughts, which the patient tries hard to resist because he or she *believes they are irrational*, and does not like them. 'The religious person who is continually tormented by sacrilegious thoughts and who may, to his great consternation, even feel himself forced to make blasphemous statements; the woman who experiences thoughts related to injuring her husband or children; men who continually fight against thoughts of homosexual activities, all fall into this category' (Malamud, 1944).

Not surprisingly, such patients are also often depressed, but the category, though small, is very varied: patients who are obsessed by cleanliness, or by particular sources of contamination, or by the dangers of things left undone, and have compulsions like incessant washing of hands or objects, or repeated 'checking rituals', such as testing locks or taps or making sure the electricity is turned off, do not always struggle against the illogicality of their concerns as much as they are supposed to. The onset of these syndromes is usually gradual, and by the time a patient has attracted clinical attention, the prognosis is generally poor – the patients are extremely resistant to psychotherapy and are occasionally recommended (by psychiatrists, not behaviour therapists) for electro-convulsive treatment and leucotomies (brain operations).

Obsessional patients may thus clearly have irrational thoughts as a main symptom, but it does not follow that cognitive methods can easily be used, in the sense of rationally arguing the patient out of the obsession. A number of procedures, of greater or lesser forcefulness than reasonable discussion, have been used by behaviour therapists in the treatment of obsessions and compulsions.

Thought stopping

Wolpe (1958) notes that obsessional thoughts and behaviours are often variable in detail, and that although in a given patient various symptoms tend to lead to one or other kind of result, obsessions can be either anxiety-elevating (exhibitionism of all kinds and intrusive thoughts) or (in the short term) anxiety-reducing (checking, washing, tidying, collecting, list-making). Other symptoms include excessive slowness (sixty minutes over shaving) and indecisiveness, and so the analysis of the causes of obsessions is complicated. As far as treatment goes, Wolpe has 'correcting misconceptions' as 'often an essential precondition to psychotherapeutic success' (1958, p. 200), but does not set much store by it and has as another subsidiary method 'thought stopping'. This is a direct and symptomatic treatment of obtrusive ruminations. The patient indicates when he is having one of these and the therapist then yells 'Stop!' and perhaps bangs the table. The patient then himself does the yelling, eventually sub-vocally, and if this is practised assiduously, it sometimes works. The patient can also be encouraged just to 'think of something else' when unwanted ideas occur, but Beech and Vaughan (1978) and Rachman and Hodgson (1980) conclude that the results obtained by these methods have usually been unreliable in clinical practice.

Exposure, flooding and response prevention

For the treatment of patients with severe and incapacitating behavioural symptoms associated with obsessions, behaviour therapists have evolved procedures in which strict and demanding requirements are imposed on those involved (mainly on the patient, but also on the therapists and their assistants, and sometimes on relatives as well). All the treatments involve exposure to disturbing circumstances, and most require the patient not to do the things he or she normally does when disturbed. In the most thorough method, that of response-prevention as used by Meyer at the Middlesex Hospital, patients are taken off all medication and put under the constant round-the-clock supervision of nursing staff and volunteers, with the aim of completely preventing them from indulging in their rituals over a period of days or weeks. Reassurance, social pressure and encouragement by the supervisors, and of course the patients' own efforts at self-control, are necessary. It is curious that Meyer (1966) originally referred to this procedure as 'modification of expectations' since the idea was to demonstrate to the patients that they were capable of surviving without their rituals, and that neither the imagined exterior events, of disease, plagues and dire accidents, often expected to affect both the patients and others in the absence of their rituals, *nor* any unacceptable increase in their own anxiety, would befall them. Subsequently Meyer has come to believe that rigorous prevention of symptomatic behaviours is, by itself, the main point to concentrate on (Meyer *et al.*, 1974).

This treatment was apparently successful and long-lasting, for during follow-ups, depression, anxiety and ability to work all showed improvements in the absence of rituals, although sexual problems tended not to show any improvement. However, it is costly in time and effort. Home visits, and homework by the patients themselves, are used by the Middlesex team, and others have reported some success with less direct attempts to prevent unwanted responses.

Absence of cleaning, checking and avoiding rituals is usually the main goal, but exposure to exaggerated or normal circumstances with less supervisory effort is often beneficial. For normal conditions the patient is simply told to 'practise therapeutic tasks in his natural environment' (Emmelkamp, 1982). They have to go home and try not to clean their hands a hundred times a day. The subtleties of this are that the therapist may assist in constructing a sequence of goals according to difficulty (90 the first day, 80 the second) and may enlist the help of family members, who are often bound up in the obsession (doing the dirty jobs, or having to wash their own hands excessively to pacify the patient). For exaggerated conditions, a patient obsessed with the possibility of contamination from animals may be required to endure the company of several dogs and cats for long periods, without subsequent decontaminatory rituals. It has been found that initially just as great an effect is obtained if the patient watches a therapist playing with dogs and cats, or putting hamsters in his or her hair, or touching doorknobs, leaving taps running or handling raw meat. This is termed 'modelling' by the therapists and appears to be a benign alternative to 'flooding' or 'satiation', in which it is the patient who must put up with excesses of this kind.

Rachman and Hodgson (1980) report success rates of between 70 and 80 per cent with procedures like this, in which patients are directly encouraged not to engage in rituals, and some success is also reported in chivvying methods of speeding up obsessive slowness. Although Meyer's rigorous response-prevention methods have been very effective, Rachman and Hodgson (1980) suggest that in future developments 'The methods of cognitive behaviour therapy are likely to be helpful'. Their clinical experience has led them to conclude that they should attempt to 'deflate the significance of obsessions' and 'try to modify the person's definition of unacceptable thoughts and impulses' (1980, p. 278). Thus, although direct methods of behaviour control have so far seemed most effective even in controlling the subjective part of obsessive-compulsive disorders, it may be that further efforts at 'cognitive restructuring' will also be useful. Checkers tend to believe that they are rational, while cleaners are more likely to admit to illogicality, and so the correcting of misconceptions in these cases may not take the same form. However it is probable that the direction of theory in behaviour therapy in both will move further in the direction of modifying expectancies, as opposed to modifying response rituals. The trinity of subjective, physiological and behavioural factors in Rachman's three-systems model already takes the theory well beyond that of simple stimulus-response alterations (Rachman and Hodgson, 1980).

Conclusion: the learning theory and behaviour modification of the future

It should be clear enough from this and previous chapters that there has in the past been a strong connection between theories of animal learning and the development of clinical and educational methods, as a matter of historical fact. Whether this was logically necessary is a different, and unanswerable, question. Perhaps Wolpe could have come up with his procedures for alleviating human anxiety without first reading Watson and Hull and doing his experiments on cats – but he didn't. It seems even less likely that the attitudes which underlie the more blinkered forms of behaviour modification would be the same if Skinner's boxes, and Skinner's writings, did not exist. Whether this historical relationship has been a good thing, or a bad thing, I leave for the reader to decide; there are many points to be made both for and against.

In my view the best single thing which practitioners in applied fields have inherited from their connection with the experimental work and scientific pretensions (to give them the least possible status) of learning theorists is their willingness to measure their successes objectively, to admit errors and to entertain new ideas. Of all forms of psychological therapy, behaviour therapy is the one where writers seem most likely to record therapeutic failures, to express doubts about their underlying theories, and to look forward to different methods which may result from new evidence and new hypotheses. This is by no means universal, of course, but I refer the reader to Rachman and Hodgson (1980) as an example. It is a necessary part of scientific pretensions that new evidence should be sought, and that old theories should be overturned, and this distinguishes the behaviour-therapy tradition from traditions based on dogmas handed down by founding gurus.

It is obvious that the main trend over the past decade has been for theories and methods of therapy to become more cognitive, that is the thoughts and feelings of both patients (or clients, or pupils) and therapists (and to a lesser extent, trainers) receive more attention. There are still arguments about this – not anymore over whether thoughts and feelings matter, but about whether they are best taken into account directly or indirectly; about whether the new approaches are as new as they seem; and about the precise way in which thoughts and feelings can be theoretically and practically related to physiological and behavioural reactions. Physiological and behavioural factors are certainly not going to disappear from the scene altogether. But in all strands of applied practice influenced by learning theory, there are hopeful anticipations of a more coherent and useful inclusion of human intellectual and emotional faculties in therapeutic methods (Rachman and Hodgson, 1980; Craighhead *et al.*, 1981; Rimm and Masters, 1979; Lowe and Higson, 1981). This is in some cases long overdue, and in all cases much to be welcomed. Irrational and counter-productive ideas, evaluations, attributions and attitudes are important components of many psychological problems, and the careful incorporation of techniques of attitude change into more behavioural techniques, which Wolpe (1958) did not ignore, will no doubt continue. Also, the principle of positive regard and human warmth towards other persons (Rogers, 1951), as well as being interpretable in terms of general encouragement and specific social reward, has much else to recommend it.

Where does this leave the connection between therapeutic methods and theories of learning which in principle apply to animal behaviour as well? To some extent, it undoubtedly leaves the connection weakened, for the future, if not for the past. But some at least of the questions and criticisms within the world of behaviour therapy were in fact thrown up first by learning theorists, not therapists (Seligman, 1970; Rachman and Seligman, 1976). These were criticisms of the over-simplified principles of conditioning as independent of species differences and independent of the detailed circumstances of individual experience. Further, just as thoughts and feelings have been surfacing in the theories of therapists, so have expectancies, evaluations and cognitive representations come to be included in theories of animal learning (Mackintosh, 1974; Dickinson, 1980; Walker, 1983). One cannot say to what degree one theoretical change has been caused by the other, but at least the changes have been occurring in synchrony which, in the separate-systems model of neurosis, is usually taken to be a healthy sign.

Suggestions for further reading

Hilgard, E.R. and Bower, G.H. (1981) *Theories of Learning*, 5th edn, Englewood Cliffs, New Jersey, Prentice-Hall (the standard work on learning theory).

Mackintosh, N.J. (1974) *The Psychology of Animal Learning*, Academic Press, London (an important reference book at the research level).

Dickinson, A. (1980) *Contemporary Animal Learning Theory*, Cambridge, Cambridge University Press (a quite difficult but short book by a leading researcher).

Gray, J.A. (1979) *Pavlov*, London, Fontana (a good general survey of Pavlov and his work in a cheap paperback).

Walker, S.F. (1983) *Animal Thought*, London, Routledge & Kegan Paul (for more on cognition in animal learning).

Two short articles by Wolpe provide useful summaries of the ideas of a major pioneer of behaviour therapy:

Wolpe, J. (1978) 'Cognition and causation in human behavior and therapy', *American Psychologist*, 33, 437–46.

Wolpe, J. (1981) 'Behavior therapy versus psychoanalysis', *American Psychologist*, 36, 159–64.

Rachman, S. (1978) *Fear and Courage*, San Francisco, Freeman (easy-to-read introduction to current ideas in behaviour therapy).

Davey, G. (ed.) (1981) *Applications of Conditioning Theory*, London, Methuen (a convenient paperback source for recent accounts of the applications of Skinnerian ideas).
Mahoney, M.J. (1983) *Cognition and Behaviour Modification*, London, Harper & Row (a classic study of cognition, now in paperback).
Craighead, W.E., Kazdin, A.E. and Mahoney, M.J. (eds) (1981) *Behavior Modification: Principles, Issues and Applications*, 2nd edn, Boston, Houghton-Mifflin (a comprehensive American textbook).

References and name index

The numbers in italics following each entry refer to page numbers in this book.

Abramson, L.Y., Seligman, M.E.P. and Teasdale, J.D. (1978) 'Learned helplessness in humans: critique and reformulation', *Journal of Abnormal Psychology*, 87, 49–74. *71*

Adams, C.D. and Dickinson, A. (1981a) 'Instrumental responding following reinforcer devaluation', *Quarterly Journal of Experimental Psychology: Comparative and Physiological Psychology*, 33B, 109–21. *49*

Adams, C.D. and Dickinson, A. (1981b) 'Actions and habits: variations in associative representations during instrumental learning', in Spear, N.E. and Miller, R.R. (eds) *Information Processing in Animals*, Hillsdale, New Jersey, Lawrence Erlbaum, 143–65. *49, 60*

Adams, R.M. and Walker, S.F. (1972) 'Stimulus control of counting-like behaviour in rats', *Psychonomic Science*, 29, 167–9. *55*

American Psychological Association (1980) 'Distinguished Scientific Award for the Application of Psychology: 1979, Joseph Wolpe', *American Psychologist*, 35, 44–51. *108*

Asratian, E.A. (1953) *I.P. Pavlov, His Life and Work*, Moscow, Foreign Languages Publishing House. *42*

Atthowe, J.M. and Krasner, L. (1968) 'Preliminary report on the applica-

tion of contingent reinforcement procedures (token economy) on a "chronic" psychiatric ward', *Journal of Abnormal Psychology*, 73, 37–43. *143*
Augustine, St, Bishop of Hippo (1929) *St Augustine's Confessions*, London, Dent (Everyman). *131*
Ayllon, T. and Azrin, N.H. (1968) *The Token Economy: A Motivational System for Therapy and Rehabilitation*, New York, Appleton-Century-Crofts. *143*
Azrin, N.H. and Foxx, R.M. (1971) 'A rapid method of toilet training of the institutionalized retarded', *Journal of Applied Behavior Analysis*, 4, 89–99. *139*
Bandura, A. (1973) *Aggression: A Social Learning Analysis*, London, Prentice-Hall. *90*
Baron, A., Dewaard, R.T. and Lipson, J. (1977) 'Increased reinforcement when time-out from avoidance includes access to a safe place', *Journal of the Experimental Analysis of Behavior*, 27, 479–94. *66*
Barr, R.F. and McConaghy, N. (1972) 'A general factor of conditionability: a study of galvanic skin response and penile responses', *Behaviour Research and Therapy*, 10, 215–27. *40*
Barton, E.S. (1975) 'Behaviour modification in the hospital school for the severely subnormal', in Kiernan, C.C. and Woodford, F.P. (eds) *Behaviour Modification with the Severely Retarded*, Amsterdam, Associated Scientific Publishers, 213–36. *139–40*
Beck, A. (1976) *Cognitive Therapy and Emotional Disorders*, New York, International Universities Press. *152*
Beech, H.R. and Vaughan, M. (1978) *Behavioural Treatment of Obsessional States*, Chichester, Wiley. *157*
Beritoff, J.S. (1971) *Vertebrate Memory*, New York, Plenum Press. *61*
Blackman, D.E. (1982) 'Psychologists and the community: influence and counter-influence', *Bulletin of the British Psychological Society*, 35, 334–41. *147*
Bolles, R.C. (1978) 'The role of stimulus learning in defensive behavior', in Hulse, S.H., Fowler, H. and Honig, W.K. (eds) *Cognitive Processes in Animal Behavior*, Hillsdale, New Jersey, Lawrence Erlbaum, 89–108. *66*
Bovee, E.C. and Lahn, J.L. (1973) 'Locomotion and behaviour', in Jeon, K.W. (ed.) *Biology of Amoeba*, London, Academic Press, 259–90. *24*
Brown, G.E. and Dixon, P.H. (1983) 'Learned helplessness in the gerbil?', *Journal of Comparative Psychology*, 97, 90–2. *71*
Brown, J.S. (1969) 'Factors affecting self-punitive locomotor behavior', in Campbell, B.A. and Church, R.M. (eds) *Punishment and Aversive Behavior*, New York, Appleton-Century-Crofts, 467–514. *69*
Brown, P.L. and Jenkins, H.M. (1968) 'Autoshaping of the pigeon's keypeck', *Journal of the Experimental Analysis of Behavior*, 11, 1–8. *50*

Callias, M. and Carr, J. (1975) 'Behaviour modification programmes in a community setting', in Kiernan, C.C. and Woodford, F.P. (eds) *Behaviour Modification in the Severely Retarded*, Amsterdam, Associated Scientific Publishers, 147–73. *142*

Cerella, J. (1979) 'Visual classes and natural categories in the pigeon', *Journal of Experimental Psychology: Human Perception and Performance*, 5, 68–77. *59*

Chomsky, N. (1959) 'Review of Skinner's *Verbal Behavior*', *Language*, 35, 26–58. *124–6*

Chomsky, N. (1965) *Aspects of the Theory of Syntax*, Cambridge, Mass., MIT Press. *140*

Chomsky, N. (1976) *Reflections on Language*, London, Fontana. *124, 126*

Chomsky, N. (1980) *Rules and Representations*, New York, Columbia University Press. *126*

Church, R.M. (1969) 'Response suppression', in Campbell, B.A. and Church, R.M. (eds) *Punishment and Aversive Behavior*, New York, Appleton-Century-Crofts, 111–56. *63–4*

Cohen, D. (1979) *J.B. Watson, the Founder of Behaviourism*, London, Routledge & Kegan Paul. *25, 81–4*

Coltheart, M. and Harris, M. (1983) *An Introduction to the Psychology of Language*, London, Routledge & Kegan Paul. *132*

Craighead, W.E., Kazdin, A.E. and Mahoney, M.J. (1981) *Behavior Modification: Principles, Issues and Applications*, 2nd edn, Boston, Houghton-Mifflin. *142, 144, 160*

Crystal, D. (1979) *Working with LARSP. Studies in Language Disability and Remediation 1A*, London, Edward Arnold. *141*

Darwin, C. (1968) *The Origin of Species*, Harmondsworth, Middlesex, Penguin (originally published, 1859). *3*

Darwin, C. (1901) *The Descent of Man and Selection in Relation to Sex*, London, John Murray (originally published, 1871). *3*

Davis, P. (1976) 'Conditioning after-images: a procedure minimizes the extinction effect of normal test trials', *British Journal of Psychology*, 67, 181–9. *41*

DiCara, L.V. and Miller, N.E. (1968) 'Changes in heart rate instrumentally learned by curarized rats as avoidance responses', *Journal of Comparative and Physiological Psychology*, 65, 8–12. *57*

Dickinson, A. (1980) *Contemporary Animal Learning Theory*, Cambridge, Cambridge University Press. *2, 16, 33, 45, 48–9, 58, 160*

Ellis, A. (1962) *Reason and Emotion in Psychotherapy*, Secausus, New Jersey, Lyle Stuart. *150, 152*

Ellis, A. (1971) *Growth Through Reason: Verbatim Cases in Rational Emotive Therapy*, Palo Alto, California, Science and Behavior Books. *152*

Emmelkamp, P. (1982) 'Recent developments in the behavioural treatment of obsessive-compulsive disorders', in Boulougouris, J.C. (ed.)

Learning Theory Approaches to Psychiatry, Chichester, Wiley, 119–28. *158*
Eysenck, H.J. (ed.) (1960) *Behaviour Therapy and the Neuroses: Modern Methods of Treatment Derived from Learning Theory*, Oxford, Pergamon Press. *110, 112*
Eysenck, H.J. (1975) 'A note on backward conditioning', *Behaviour Research and Therapy*, 13, 201. *43*
Eysenck, H.J. (1976) 'The learning theory model of neurosis – a new approach', *Behaviour Research and Therapy*, 14, 251–67. *113, 120*
Eysenck, H.J. (1979) 'The conditioning model of neurosis', *Behavioral and Brain Sciences*, 2, 155–99. *121*
Ferster, C.B. and Skinner, B.F. (1957) *Schedules of Reinforcement*, New York, Appleton-Century-Crofts. *50, 53–5*
Findley, J.D. and Brady, J.V. (1965) 'Facilitation of large ratio performance by use of conditioned reinforcement', *Journal of the Experimental Analysis of Behavior*, 8, 125–9. *55*
Fowler, H. and Wischner, G.J. (1969) 'The varied effects of punishment on discrimination learning', in Campbell, B.A. and Church, R.M. (eds) *Punishment and Aversive Behavior*, New York, Appleton-Century-Crofts, 375–420. *70*
Fuller, P.R. (1949) 'Operant conditioning of a vegetative human organism', *American Journal of Psychology*, 62, 587–90.
Garcia, J. (1981) 'Tilting at the paper mills of academe', *American Psychologist*, 36, 149–58. *49, 68*
Garcia, J., Ervin, F.R. and Koelling, R.A. (1966) 'Learning with prolonged delay of reinforcement', *Psychonomic Science*, 5, 121–2. *68*
Garcia, J. and Koelling, R.A. (1966) 'Relation of cue to consequence in avoidance learning', *Psychonomic Science*, 4, 123–4. *68*
Garcia, J., Rusinak, K.W. and Brett, L.P. (1977) 'Conditioning food-illness aversions in wild animals: caveant canonici', in Davis, H. and Hurwitz, H.M.B. (eds) *Operant-Pavlovian Interactions*, Hillsdale, New Jersey, Lawrence Erlbaum, 273–316. *68–9*
Glazer, H.I. and Weiss, J.M. (1976) 'Long term interference effect: an alternative to "learned helplessness"', *Journal of Experimental Psychology: Animal Behavior Processes*, 2, 212–13. *72*
Gray, J.A. (1975) *Elements of a Two-Process Theory of Learning*, London, Academic Press. *42, 67*
Gray, J.A. (1979) *Pavlov*, London, Fontana. *36, 73, 79*
Gray, J.A. (1982) *The Neuropsychology of Anxiety; An Examination of the Functions of the Septo-Hippocampal System*, London, Oxford University Press. *115*
Halmi, K.A., Powers, P. and Cunningham, S. (1975) 'Treatment of anorexia nervosa with behavior modification', *Archives of General Psychiatry*, 32, 93–6. *142*

Harris, B. (1979) 'Whatever happened to Little Albert?', *American Psychologist*, 34, 151–60. *83, 88*
Harris, M., Jones, D. and Grant, J. (1983) 'The nonverbal context of mothers' speech to infants', *First Language*, 4, 11–99. *130*
Haughton, E. and Ayllon, T. (1965) 'Production and elimination of symptomatic behaviors', in Ullman, L.P. and Krasner, L. (eds) *Case Studies in Behavior Modification*, New York, Holt, Rinehart & Winston, 94–8. *142*
Hayes, K.J. and Nissen, C.H. (1971) 'Higher mental functions of a home-raised chimpanzee', in Schrier, A.M. and Stolnitz, F. (eds) *Behavior of Nonhuman Primates*, 4, New York, Academic Press, 59–115. *61*
Herrnstein, R.J. (1969) 'Method and theory in the study of avoidance', *Psychological Review*, 76, 46–69. *66–7*
Herrnstein, R.J., Loveland, D.H. and Cable, C. (1976) 'Natural concepts in pigeons', *Journal of Experimental Psychology: Animal Behavior Processes*, 2, 285–302. *59*
Hilgard, E.R. and Bower, G.H. (1981) *Theories of Learning*, 5th edn, Englewood Cliffs, New Jersey, Prentice-Hall. *16*
Hinde, R.A. and Stevenson-Hinde, J. (1973) *Constraints on Learning*, London, Academic Press. 46
Hobhouse, L.T. (1901) *Mind in Evolution*, London, Macmillan. *98*
Holding, D.H. and Jones, D.D. (1976) 'Delayed one-trial extinction of the McCullough effect', *Quarterly Journal of Experimental Psychology*, 218, 683–7. *41*
Holland, P.C. and Rescorla, R.A. (1975) 'Second-order conditioning with food unconditioned stimulus', *Journal of Comparative and Physiological Psychology*, 88, 459–67. *44*
Horridge, G.A. (1962) 'Learning of leg position by the ventral nerve cord in headless insects', *Proceedings of the Royal Society Series B*, 157, 33–52. *49*
Hugdahl, K. (1981) 'The three-systems-model of fear and emotion – a critical examination', *Behaviour Research and Therapy*, 19, 75–85. *116*
Hull, C.L. (1929) 'A functional interpretation of the conditioned reflex', *Psychological Review*, 36, 498–511. *15*
Hull, C.L. (1933) *Hypnosis and Suggestibility*, New York, Appleton-Century-Crofts. *104*
Hull, C.L. (1937) 'Mind, mechanism and adaptive behavior', *Psychological Review*, 44, 1–32. *15*
Hull, C.L. (1943) *Principles of Behavior*, New York, Appleton-Century-Crofts. *14–16, 98*
Hull, C.L. (1952) *A Behavior System*, New Haven, Connecticut, Yale University Press. *14–16*
Hulse, S.H., Fowler, H. and Honig, W.K. (eds) (1978) *Cognitive Pro-*

cesses in Animal Behavior, Hillsdale, New Jersey, Lawrence Erlbaum. *58*
Hume, D. (1970) *Enquiries Concerning the Human Understanding and Concerning the Principles of Morals*, London, Oxford University Press (originally published, 1777). *26*
Huxley, A. (1983) *Brave New World*, London, Granada (originally published, 1932). *86*
Ince, L.P., Brucker, B.S. and Alba, A. (1978) 'Reflex conditioning in a spinal man', *Journal of Comparative Physiological Psychology*, 92, 796–802. *37*
James, W. (1891) *The Principles of Psychology*, London, Macmillan. *8*
Jenkins, H.M., Barrera, F.J., Ireland, C. and Woodside, B. (1978) 'Signal-centred action patterns of dogs in appetitive classical conditioning', *Learning and Motivation*, 9, 272–96. *51*
Jennings, H.S. (1906) *The Behavior of the Lower Organisms*, New York, Columbia University Press. *24*
Jones, M.C. (1924a) 'A laboratory study of fear: the case of Peter', *Pedagogical Seminary*, 31, 308–31. *89*
Jones, M.C. (1924b) 'The elimination of children's fears', *Journal of Experimental Psychology*, 7, 382–90. *89–90*
Jones, M.C. (1974) 'Albert, Peter and J.B. Watson', *American Psychologist*, 29, 581–3. *89*
Kazdin, A.E. (1977) *The Token Economy: A Review and Evaluation*, London, Plenum Press. *144*
Kazdin, A.E. (1978) *History of Behavior Modification*, Baltimore, Maryland, University Park Press. *83, 92*
Kazdin, A.E. (1981) 'The token economy', in Davey, G. (ed.) *Applications of Conditioning Theory*, London, Methuen, 59–80. *144*
Keith-Lukas, J. and Guttman, N. (1975) 'Robust single-trial delayed backward conditioning', *Journal of Comparative and Physiological Psychology*, 88, 468–76. *42–3*
Kesner, R.P. and Cook, D.G. (1983) 'Role of habituation and classical conditioning in the development of morphine tolerance', *Behavioral Neuroscience*, 97, 4–12. *38*
Kiernan, C.C. and Woodford, F.P. (eds) (1975) *Behaviour Modification with the Severely Retarded*, Amsterdam, Associated Scientific Publishers. *138*
Lea, S.E.G. (1984) *Instinct, Environment and Behaviour*, London, Methuen. *25, 51, 58*
Ledwidge, B. (1978) 'Cognitive behavior modification: a step in the wrong direction', *Psychological Bulletin*, 85, 353–75. *148–9, 151*
Lenneberg, E. (1967) *Biological Foundations of Language*, New York, Wiley. *124, 140*
Levey, A.B. and Martin, I. (1975) 'Classical conditioning of human

evaluative response', *Behavioural Research and Therapy*, 13, 221–6. *41–2*
Lewin, K. (1935) *A Dynamic Theory of Personality*, New York, McGraw-Hill. *95*
Lowe, C.F. and Higson, P.J. (1981) 'Self-instruction training and cognitive behaviour modification: a behavioural analysis', in Davey, G. (ed.) *Applications of Conditioning Theory*, London, Methuen, 162–88. *147, 160*
Luria, A.R. (1961) *The Role of Speech in the Regulation of Normal and Abnormal Behaviour*, Oxford, Pergamon Press. *153*
Luria, A.R. (1966) *Higher Cortical Functions in Man*, London, Tavistock. *74*
Lutzker, J.R. and Sherman, J.A. (1974) 'Producing generative sentence usage by imitation and reinforcement procedures', *Journal of Applied Behavior Analysis*, 7, 447–60. *140*
McCullough, C. (1965) 'Colour adaptation of edge detectors in the human visual system', *Science*, 149, 1115–16. *41*
Mackintosh, N.J. (1974) *The Psychology of Animal Learning*, London, Academic Press. *16, 27, 33, 45, 48, 51, 58, 60, 64, 67, 160*
Magee, B. (1975) *Popper*, London, Fontana. *24*
Mahoney, M.J. (1974) *Cognition and Behavior Modification*, Cambridge, Mass., Ballinger. *118, 145*
Mahoney, M.J. (1983) *Cognition and Behavior Modification*, London, Harper & Row.
Malamud, W. (1944) 'The psychoneuroses', in Hunt, J. McV. (ed.) *Personality and the Behavior Disorders*, 2, New York, Ronald Press, 833–60. *155*
Maudsley, H. (1876) *The Physiology of Mind*, 3rd edn, London, Macmillan. *112*
Maudsley, H. (1979) *The Pathology of Mind*, London, Julian Friedmann (originally published, 1895). *111–12*
Medin, D.L., Roberts, W.A. and Davis, R.T. (eds) (1976) *Processes of Animal Memory*, Hillsdale, New Jersey, Lawrence Erlbaum. *60*
Meichenbaum, D. (1977) *Cognitive Behavior Modification: An Interactive Approach*, New York, Plenum Press. *121, 145, 153–4*
Melvin, K.B. and Smith, F.H. (1967) 'Self-punitive avoidance behavior in the rat', *Journal of Comparative and Physiological Psychology*, 63, 533–5. *70*
Menzel, E.W. (1978) 'Cognitive mapping in chimpanzees', in Hulse, S.H., Fowler, H. and Honig, W.K. (eds) *Cognitive Processes in Animal Behavior*, Hillsdale, New Jersey, Lawrence Erlbaum, 373–422. *61*
Meyer, V. (1957) 'The treatment of two phobic patients on the basis of learning principles', *Journal of Abnormal and Social Psychology*, 55, 261–6. *112*

Meyer, V. (1966) 'Modifications of expectations in cases with obsessional rituals', *Behaviour Research and Therapy*, 4, 273–80. *157*

Meyer, V., Levy, R. and Schurer, A. (1974) 'The behavioural treatment of obsessive-compulsive disorders', in Beech, H.R. (ed.) *Obsessional States*, London, Methuen, 233–58. *157*

Migler, B. (1963) 'Experimental self-punishment and superstitious escape behavior', *Journal of the Experimental Analysis of Behavior*, 6, 371–81. *70*

Miller, I.W. and Norman, W.H. (1979) 'Learned helplessness in humans: a review and attribution theory model', *Psychological Bulletin*, 86, 93–118. *71–2*

Miller, N.E. (1944) 'Experimental studies of conflict', in Hunt, J.McV. (ed.) *Personality and the Behavior Disorders*, New York, Ronald Press, 413–30. *65*

Miller, N.E. (1948) 'Studies of fear as an acquirable drive', *Journal of Experimental Psychology*, 38, 89–101. *67*

Miller, N.E. (1978) 'Biofeedback and visceral learning', *Annual Review of Psychology*, 29, 373–404. *57*

Miller, N.E. and DiCara, L.V. (1967) 'Instrumental learning of heart-rate changes in curarised rats: shaping and specificity to discriminative stimulus', *Journal of Comparative and Physiological Psychology*, 63, 12–19. *57*

Molliver, M.E. (1963) 'Operant control of vocal behavior in the cat', *Journal of the Experimental Analysis of Behavior*, 6, 197–202. *155*

Morgan, M.J., Fitch, M.D., Holman, J.G. and Lea, S.E.G. (1976) 'Pigeons learn the concept of an "A"', *Perception*, 5, 57–66. *59*

Mowrer, O.H. (1969) 'Psychoneurotic defenses (including deception) as punishment avoidance strategies', in Campbell, B.A. and Church, R.M. (eds) *Punishment and Aversive Behavior*, New York, Appleton-Century-Crofts, 449–66. *67*

Mowrer, O.H. (1980) 'Enuresis – the beginning work. What really happened', *Journal of the History of the Behavioral Sciences*, 16, 25–30. *99*

Muenzinger, K.F. (1934) 'Motivation in learning. I. Electric shock for correct responses in the visual discrimination habit', *Journal of Comparative Psychology*, 17, 267–77. *70*

Nussbaum, M.C. (1978) *Aristotle's De Motu Animalium*, Princeton, New Jersey, Princeton University Press. *23*

Oakley, D.A. (1979) 'Cerebral cortex and adaptive behaviour', in Oakley, D.A. and Plotkin, H.C. (eds) *Brain, Behaviour and Evolution*, London, Methuen, 154–88. *37, 48–9*

Ohman, A., Ericksonn, G. and Lofberg, I. (1975) 'Phobias and preparedness: phobic versus neutral pictures as conditioned stimuli for human autonomic responses', *Journal of Abnormal Psychology*, 84, 41–5. *39*

O'Keefe, J. and Nadel, L. (1978) *The Hippocampus as a Cognitive Map*, Oxford, Clarendon Press. *58*

Olton, D.S. (1979) 'Mazes, maps, and memory', *American Psychologist*, 34, 583–96. *58*

Overman, W.H. and Doty, R.W. (1980) 'Prolonged visual memory in macaques and man', *Neuroscience*, 5, 1825–31. *60*

Pavlov, I.P. (1927) *Conditioned Reflexes: An Investigation of the Physiological Activity of the Cerebral Cortex*, New York, Dover. *6, 7, 26, 32–7, 76–9*

Pavlov, I.P. (1955) *Selected Works*, Moscow, Foreign Languages Publishing House. *73–9*

Pavlov, I.P. (1962) *Psychopathology and Psychiatry*, edited by Y. Popov and L. Rokhlin, Moscow, Foreign Languages Publishing House. *74*

Peters, R.H. (1983) 'Learned aversions to copulatory behaviors in male rats', *Behavioral Neuroscience*, 97, 140–5. *68*

Pieper, A. (1963) *Cerebral Function in Infancy and Childhood*, London, Pitman. *88*

Popper, K.R. (1972) *Objective Knowledge*, London, Oxford University Press. *24*

Rachman, S. (1966) 'Sexual fetishism: an experimental analogue', *Psychological Record*, 16, 293–6. *40*

Rachman, S. (1977) 'The conditioning theory of fear-acquisition: a critical examination', *Behaviour Research and Therapy*, 15, 375–87. *118–20*

Rachman, S. (1978) *Fear and Courage*, San Francisco, Freeman. *116, 118–19*

Rachman, S. (1981) 'The primacy of affect: some theoretical implications', *Behaviour Research and Therapy*, 19, 279–90. *118*

Rachman, S. and Hodgson, R. (1968) 'Experimentally induced fetishism: replication and development', *Psychological Record*, 18, 25–7. *40*

Rachman, S. and Hodgson, R. (1980) *Obsessions and Compulsions*, Englewood Cliffs, New Jersey, Prentice-Hall. *157–60*

Rachman, S. and Seligman, M.E.P. (1976) 'Unprepared phobias; "be prepared"', *Behaviour Research and Therapy*, 14, 333–8. *160*

Rescorla, R.A. (1978) 'Some implications of a cognitive perspective on Pavlovian conditioning', in Hulse, S.H., Fowler, H. and Honig, W.K. (eds) *Cognitive Processes in Animal Behavior*, Hillsdale, New Jersey, Lawrence Erlbaum. *36*

Rescorla, R.A. (1979) 'Aspects of the reinforcer learned in second-order Pavlovian conditioning', *Journal of Experimental Psychology: Animal Behavior Processes*, 5, 79–95. *33*

Rescorla, R.A. (1980) *Pavlovian Second-Order Conditioning*, Hillsdale, New Jersey, Lawrence Erlbaum. *2, 43*

Rescorla, R.A. and Wagner, A.R. (1972) 'A theory of Pavlovian condition-

ing: variations in the effectiveness of reinforcement and non-reinforcement', in Black, A.H. and Prokasy, W.F. (eds) *Classical Conditioning*, 2, New York, Appleton-Century-Crofts, 64–99. *16*
Rimm, D.C. and Masters, J.C. (1979) *Behaviour Therapy: Techniques and Empirical Findings*, 2nd edn, London, Academic Press. *160*
Roberts, R. and Church, R.M. (1978) 'Control of an eternal clock', *Journal of Experimental Psychology: Animal Behavior Processes*, 4, 318–37. *53*
Rogers, C.R. (1951) *Client-Centered Therapy*, Boston, Houghton-Mifflin. *160*
Roitblat, H.L., Bever, T.G. and Terrace, H.S. (eds) (1983) *Animal Cognition*, Hillsdale, New Jersey, Lawrence Erlbaum. *58, 60*
Roosevelt, F.D. (1933) 'Inaugural speech', 4 March, Washington, DC (quoted in Cohen, J.M. and Cohen, M.J. (eds) (1960) *The Penguin Dictionary of Quotations*, Harmondsworth, Penguin). *114*
Rosenfeld, H.M. and Baer, D.M. (1969) 'Unnoticed verbal conditioning of an aware experimenter by a more aware subject: the double-agent effect', *Psychological Review*, 76, 425–32. *49*
Samuelson, F. (1980) 'J.B. Watson's Little Albert, Cyril Burt's twins, and the need for a critical science', *American Psychologist*, 35, 619–25. *83, 88*
Sechenov, I.M. (1973) *Selected Works*, New York, Arno Press (originally published, 1863).
Seligman, M.E.P. (1970) 'On the generality of the laws of learning', *Psychological Review*, 77, 406–18. *23, 46, 114, 160*
Seligman, M.E.P. (1975) *Helplessness: On Depression, Development and Death*, San Francisco, Freeman. *23, 71, 76*
Seligman, M.E.P. and Beagley, G. (1975), 'Learned helplessness in the rat', *Journal of Comparative and Physiological Psychology*, 88, 534–41. *71*
Seligman, M.E.P., Maier, S.F. and Geer, J.H. (1968) 'Alleviation of learned helplessness in the dog', *Journal of Abnormal Psychology*, 73, 256–62. *71, 115*
Shettleworth, S.J. and Krebs, J.R. (1982) 'How marsh tits find their hoards: the roles of site preference and spatial memory', *Journal of Experimental Psychology: Animal Behavior Processes*, 8, 354–75. *61*
Sidman, M. (1953) 'Avoidance conditioning with brief shock and no exteroceptive signal', *Science*, 118, 157–8. *66*
Siegel, S. (1976) 'Morphine analgesic tolerance: its situation-specificity supports a Pavlovian conditioning model', *Science*, 193, 323–5. *38*
Skinner, B.F. (1931) 'The concept of a reflex in the description of behavior', *Journal of General Psychology*, 5, 427–58. *12*
Skinner, B.F. (1935) 'Two types of conditioned reflex and a pseudo-type', *Journal of General Psychology*, 12, 66–77. *13*

Skinner, B.F. (1938) *The Behavior of Organisms*, New York, Appleton-Century-Crofts. *13, 46*
Skinner, B.F. (1948) *Walden Two*, New York, Macmillan (reprinted, 1962). *132–4*
Skinner, B.F. (1950) 'Are theories of learning necessary?', *Psychological Review*, 57, 193–216. *14*
Skinner, B.F. (1953) *Science and Human Behavior*, New York, Macmillan. *64, 137*
Skinner, B.F. (1957) *Verbal Behavior*, New York, Appleton-Century-Crofts. *124–9*
Skinner, B.F. (1972) *Beyond Freedom and Dignity*, London, Jonathan Cape. *132, 136*
Skinner, B.F. (1974) *About Behaviourism*, London, Jonathan Cape.
Skinner, B.F. (1983) 'Intellectual self-management in old age', *American Psychologist*, 38, 239–54. *135*
Sokolov, A.N. (1972) *Inner Speech and Thought*, New York, Plenum. *153*
Solomon, R.L. (1964) 'Punishment', *American Psychologist*, 19, 237–53. *63*
Solomon, R.L., Kamin, L.J. and Wynne, L.C. (1953) 'Traumatic avoidance learning: the outcomes of several extinction procedures with dogs', *Journal of Abnormal and Social Psychology*, 48, 291–302. *63, 70, 115*
Solomon, R.L. and Wynne, L.C. (1954) 'Traumatic avoidance learning: the principle of anxiety conservation and partial irreversibility', *Psychological Review*, 61, 653–85.
Spence, K.W. and Lippsit, R. (1946) 'An experimental test of the sign-Gestalt theory of trial-and-error learning', *Journal of Experimental Psychology*, 36, 491–502. *28*
Spencer, H.S. (1899) *The Principles of Psychology*, 4th edn, London, Williams & Norgate (first published 1855). *26, 112*
Steptoe, A. (1981) *Psychological Factors in Cardiovascular Disorders*, London, Academic Press.
Stevens-Long, J. and Rasmussen, M. (1974) 'The acquisition of simple and compound sentence structure in an autistic child', *Journal of Applied Behavior Analysis*, 7, 473–9. *140*
Stokes, T.F., Baer, D.M. and Jackson, R.L. (1974) 'Programming the generalization of a greeting response in four retarded children', *Journal of Applied Behavior Analysis*, 7, 599–610. *141*
Stolz, S.B., Wienckowski, L.A. and Brown, B.S. (1975) 'Behavior modification: a perspective on critical issues', *American Psychologist*, 30, 1027–48. *138, 144*
Tennant, L., Cullen, C., and Hattersley, J. (1981) 'Applied behaviour analysis: intervention with retarded people', in Davey, G. (ed.) *Applications of Conditioning Theory*, London, Methuen, 29–58.
Terlecki, L.J., Pinel, J.P.L. and Treit, D. (1979) 'Conditioned and

unconditioned defensive burying in the rat', *Learning and Motivation*, 10, 337–50. *69*

Terrace, H.S. (1981) 'Introduction: autoshaping and two factor learning theory', in Locurto, C.M., Terrace, H.S. and Gibbon, J. (eds) *Autoshaping and Conditioning Theory*, London, Academic Press, 1–18. *50*

Thorndike, E.L. (1898) 'Animal intelligence: an experimental study of the associative processes in animals', *Psychological Review, Monograph Supplements*, 2 (8), 1–109. *8–10, 47–8, 93–4*

Thorndike, E.L. (1901) 'The mental life of the monkeys', *Psychological Review, Monograph Supplements*, 3 (5), 1–57. *93*

Thorndike, E.L. (1907) *The Elements of Psychology*, 2nd edn, New York, A.G. Seiler (first published, 1905). *12, 95*

Thorndike, E.L. (1913) *Educational Psychology*, 1, New York, Teachers College.

Thorndike, E.L. (1931) *Human Learning*, London, Century. *94*

Thorndike, E.L. (1932) 'Reward and punishment in animal learning', *Comparative Psychology Monographs*, 8 (39), 1–23. *64*

Thorndike, E.L. and Lorge, I. (1944) *The Teacher's Word Book of 30,000 Words*, New York, Teachers College. *94*

Thorpe, J.G. (1975) 'Token economy systems', in Kiernan, C.C. and Woodford, F.P. (eds) *Behaviour Modification in the Severely Retarded*, Amsterdam, Associated Scientific Publishers, 249–59. *144*

Timberlake, W. and Grant, D.L. (1975) 'Autoshaping rats to the presentation of another rat predicting food', *Science*, 190, 690–2. *51–2*

Tolman, E.C. (1922) 'A new formula for behaviorism', *Psychological Review*, 29, 44–53. *16*

Tolman, E.C. (1925) 'Purpose and cognition: the determiners of animal learning', *Psychological Review*, 32, 285–97. *17*

Tolman, E.C. (1926) 'A behaviorist theory of ideas', *Psychological Review*, 33, 352–69. *17*

Tolman, E.C. (1942) *Drives Towards War*, London, Appleton-Century-Crofts. *96*

Tolman, E.C. (1948) 'Cognitive maps in rats and men', *Psychological Review*, 55, 189–208. *17–19, 97*

Tolman, E.C. (1951) *Collected Papers in Psychology*, Berkeley, University of California Press. *17*

Tolman, E.C. (1959) 'Principles of purposive behaviourism', in Koch, S. (ed.) *Psychology: A Study of a Science, Study 1*, 2, London, McGraw-Hill, 92–157.

Tolman, E.C. and Honzik, C.H. (1930) 'Introduction and removal of reward, and maze learning in rats', *University of California Publications in Psychology*, 4, 257–75. *18–20*

Vygotsky, L.S. (1962) *Thought and Language*, New York, Wiley (originally published, 1934). *153*
Wahler, R.G. (1969) 'Oppositional children: a quest for parental reinforcement control', *Journal of Applied Behavior Analysis*, 2, 159–270. *142, 154*
Wahler, R.G. (1980) 'The insular mother: her problems in parent–child treatment', *Journal of Applied Behavior Analysis*, 13, 207–19. *154*
Walker, S.F. (1975) 'Current laboratory analyses of behaviour and behaviour modification', in Kiernan, C.C. and Woodford, F.P. (eds) *Behaviour Modification with the Severely Retarded*, Amsterdam, Associated Scientific Publishers, 119–43. *58*
Walker, S.F. (1983) *Animal Thought*, London, Routledge & Kegan Paul. *16, 25, 58–61, 160*
Walters, E.T., Carew, T.J. and Kandel, E.R. (1981) 'Associative learning in *Aplysia*: Evidence for conditioned fear in an invertebrate', *Science*, 211, 504–6. *32*
Watson, J.B. (1903) *Animal Education*, Chicago, University of Chicago Press. *11*
Watson, J.B. (1913) 'Psychology as the behaviourist views it', *Psychological Review*, 20, 158–77. *10–12*
Watson, J.B. (1914) *Behaviour: An Introduction to Comparative Psychology*, London, Holt, Rinehart, & Winston (reprinted, 1967). *10, 24, 81*
Watson, J.B. (1931) *Behaviourism*, 2nd edn, London, Kegan Paul, Trench & Trubner. *10–12, 80, 84–9*
Watson, J.B. and Rayner, R. (1920) 'Conditioned emotional reactions', *Journal of Experimental Psychology*, 3, 1–4.
Weismann, R.G., Wasserman, E.A., Dodd, P.W.D. and Larew, M.B. (1980) 'Representation and retention of two-event sequences in pigeons', *Journal of Experimental Psychology: Animal Behavior Processes*, 6, 312–25. *60*
Williams, C.D. (1959) 'The elimination of tantrum behaviour by extinction procedures', *Journal of Abnormal and Social Psychology*, 59, 269. *141*
Williams, D.R. and Williams, H. (1969) 'Automaintenance in the pigeon, sustained pecking despite contingent non-reinforcement', *Journal of the Experimental Analysis of Behavior*, 12, 511–20. *51*
Wilson, E.O. (1975) *Sociobiology*, Cambridge, Mass., Harvard University Press. *4*
Wincze, J.-P., Leitenberg, H. and Agras, W.S. (1972) 'The effects of token reinforcement and feedback on the delusional verbal behavior of chronic paranoid schizophrenics', *Journal of Applied Behavior Analysis*, 5, 247–62. *154*
Wolf, M.M., Risley, T. and Mees, H. (1964) 'Application of operant

conditioning procedures to the behaviour problems of an autistic child', *Behaviour Research and Therapy*, 1, 305–12. *141*

Wolpe, J. (1952) 'Experimental neurosis as learned behaviour', *British Journal of Psychology*, 43, 243–68. *100*

Wolpe, J. (1958) *Psychotherapy by Reciprocal Inhibition*, Stanford, California, Stanford University Press. *99, 102–3, 106, 115, 156, 160*

Wolpe, J. (1976) *Theme and Variations: A Behavior Therapy Casebook*, New York Pergamon Press. *100*

Wolpe, J. (1978) 'Cognition and causation in human behavior and therapy', *American Psychologist*, 33, 437–46. *102, 108, 137, 149, 155*

Wolpe, J. (1981) 'Behavior therapy versus psychoanalysis', *American Psychologist*, 36, 159–64. *102, 108, 149*

Woods, S.C. (1976) 'Conditioned hypoglycemia', *Journal of Comparative and Physiological Psychology*, 90, 1164–8. *38*

Yates, A. (1980) *Biofeedback and the Modification of Behavior*, New York, Plenum Press. *57*

Subject index

The references section of this book serves as a name index. Names are included in this index only where there is no corresponding literature citation; in most cases these are the names of historical personages.